vegan
100 everyday recipes

First published in 2013
LOVE FOOD is an imprint of Parragon Books Ltd

Parragon
Chartist House
15-17 Trim Street
Bath BA1 1HA, UK

Copyright © Parragon Books Ltd 2013

LOVE FOOD and the accompanying heart device is a registered trade mark of Parragon Books Ltd in Australia, the UK, USA, India and the EU.

www.parragon.com/lovefood

ISBN: 978-1-4723-1083-5

Printed in China

New recipes by Jane Hughes
Cover and new internal photography by Noel Murphy
Home economy for new photography by Penny Stephens

Notes for the Reader

This book uses both metric and imperial measurements. Follow the same units of measurement throughout; do not mix metric and imperial. All spoon measurements are level: teaspoons are assumed to be 5 ml, and tablespoons are assumed to be 15 ml. Unless otherwise stated, milk is assumed to be full fat, eggs and individual vegetables are medium, and pepper is freshly ground black pepper. Unless otherwise stated, all root vegetables should be washed in plain water and peeled prior to using. Garnishes, decorations and serving suggestions are all optional and not necessarily included in the recipe ingredients or method.

The times given are an approximate guide only. Preparation times differ according to the techniques used by different people and the cooking times may also vary from those given. Optional ingredients, variations or serving suggestions have not been included in the time calculations.

Recipes using raw or very lightly cooked eggs should be avoided by infants, the elderly, pregnant women, convalescents and anyone suffering from an illness. Pregnant and breastfeeding women are advised to avoid eating peanuts and peanut products. Sufferers from nut allergies should be aware that some of the ready-made ingredients used in the recipes in this book may contain nuts. Always check the packaging before use.

Vegan Ingredients

The publisher has been careful to select recipes that do not contain animal products. Any ready-made ingredients that could potentially contain animal products have been listed as 'vegan', so readers know to look for the vegan version. However, always read labels carefully and, if necessary, check with the manufacturer. The publisher recommends consulting a doctor or other health-care professional before embarking on any major dietary changes.

vegan

introduction

Veganism is moving into the mainstream. As more and more people have chosen to be vegetarian over the past decades, interest in veganism is also growing. Unlike vegetarians, vegans prefer not to consume any food or drink that is derived from an animal. The vegan diet is free from eggs, dairy foods and even honey. In days gone by, critics of vegetarianism argued that the diet was not a healthy one and that, for the sake of our health, a balanced diet must include meat. Yet today, millions of vegetarians are thriving and research tells us that, far from being essential for our health, meat (and especially red and processed meat) is something we should aim to eat less, not more, of. For those who decide to eat less meat for either health or animal welfare reasons, going vegan is a logical step. Dairy foods are often high in fat and cholesterol, and the large-scale production of milk and eggs inevitably raises concerns about how we treat animals. The old arguments against vegetarianism, that it is a restrictive and unhealthy diet, are now levelled against veganism – but once again, the proof of the pudding is in the eating. People report that

moving to a plant-based diet has improved their health, that they feel invigorated and fit, and that they can no longer understand why they once relied on dairy foods and eggs for protein. As the world's population rockets, we must find a way to feed everybody. The answer is not to build intensive dairy farms or to genetically engineer animals to yield more milk, more eggs or more meat. The fact is that we do not need to eat food that comes from animals. If we continue to eat food from animals, it means using water and grains that could sustain many people to produce unhealthy animal-based foods that feed far fewer people. It's time to rethink our diets. A plant-based diet is sensible, healthy and better for the planet. But we're only human and we eat for enjoyment as well as fuel. Divided into sections on breakfasts, snacks, lunches, dinners and desserts, this book offers recipes for a variety of tasty dishes that everybody will enjoy. Yes, vegans can eat cake and ice cream at long last! Whether you're experimenting with vegan cuisine for the first time or looking for some fresh inspiration for an established vegan diet, these straightforward recipes are sure to become favourites.

breakfast

green apple & kiwi juice

ingredients

serves 2

2 green apples, such as Granny
    Smith
½ cucumber
2 kiwi fruits
½ lemon
2-cm/¾-inch piece fresh ginger,
    peeled

method

1 Core the apples and then chop the unpeeled flesh
   into small pieces. Dice the cucumber. Peel the kiwi
   fruit using a standard vegetable peeler and then chop
   into small pieces. Cut the lemon into thin slices and set
   two slices to one side. Finely chop the ginger using a
   sharp knife.

2 Place all of the ingredients into a juicer and juice all the
   ingredients together until all the liquid is extracted.

3 Transfer the juice to tall glasses and decorate the
   glasses with the remaining lemon slices. Serve
   immediately.

berry sunrise smoothie

ingredients

serves 1

1 banana
55 g/2 oz silken tofu, drained
175 ml/6 fl oz orange juice
200 g/7 oz frozen mixed berries

method

1 Roughly chop the banana and the tofu into smaller pieces.

2 Place all of the ingredients into a food processor or blender, or place into a large, deep bowl and use a hand-held blender. Blend gently until thoroughly combined.

3 Serve immediately in a tall drinking glass.

strawberry & vanilla soya shake

ingredients

serves 2

200 g/7 oz strawberries
200 ml/7 fl oz plain soya yogurt
100 ml/3½ fl oz chilled soya milk
2 tsp vanilla extract
agave nectar, to taste

method

1 Pick over the strawberries, then hull and halve them and place into a small bowl.

2 Place the strawberry halves, yogurt, milk and vanilla extract into a food processor or blender, or place these ingredients into a large, deep bowl and use a hand-held blender. Blend gently until thoroughly combined. Sweeten with agave nectar to taste.

3 Serve immediately in tall drinking glasses.

apricot & ginger juice

ingredients

serves 2

6 apricots
1 orange
1 fresh lemon grass stalk
2-cm/¾-inch piece fresh ginger,
    peeled
ice cubes, to serve

method

1 Halve and stone the apricots. Peel the orange, leaving some of the white pith. Cut the lemon grass into chunks.

2 Place the apricots, orange, lemon grass and ginger in a juicer and juice all the ingredients together until all the liquid is extracted. Pour the mixture into glasses, add ice and serve immediately.

red pepper booster

ingredients

serves 2

250 ml/9 fl oz carrot juice
250 ml/9 fl oz tomato juice
2 large red peppers, deseeded
    and roughly chopped
1 tbsp lemon juice
pepper
lemon slices, to garnish

method

1 Pour the carrot juice and tomato juice into a food processor or blender and process gently until combined.

2 Add the red peppers and lemon juice. Season with plenty of pepper and process until smooth. Pour the mixture into glasses, garnish with lemon slices and serve immediately.

maple & banana soya shake

ingredients

serves 2

large banana
350 ml/12 fl oz chilled soya or
    almond milk
2 tbsp vegan omega 369 oil
1 tsp maple syrup

method

1 Chop the banana and place the pieces into a
small bowl.

2 Place the banana pieces, milk and omega oil into a
food processor or blender, or place these ingredients
into a large, deep bowl and use a hand-held blender.
Blend gently until thoroughly combined. Sweeten with
maple syrup to taste.

3 Serve immediately in tall drinking glasses.

peanut butter muesli

ingredients

serves 3–4

150 g/5½ oz porridge oats
3 tbsp linseed meal (ground
    golden linseeds)
30 g/1 oz vegan margarine
40 g/1½ oz crunchy peanut butter
50 g/1¾ oz light agave nectar
½ tsp vanilla extract
soya milk or soya yogurt and
    blueberries, to serve

method

1 Preheat the oven to 160°C/325°F/Gas Mark 3. Line a baking sheet with baking paper.

2 Mix together the oats and linseed meal in a large bowl.

3 Warm the margarine, peanut butter and agave nectar together, either in a small saucepan over a low heat or in a heatproof jug in the microwave, until the margarine melts. Add the vanilla extract and mix together thoroughly.

4 Stir the liquid mixture into the oats and linseed meal in the bowl and stir well to combine.

5 Spread the oat mixture onto the prepared baking sheet and bake in the preheated oven for 20 minutes, or until dry and beginning to turn golden. Remove from the oven and allow the mixture to cool completely. Crumble the muesli and store in an airtight container or serve straightaway in bowls with soya milk or soya yogurt and fresh blueberries.

cherry almond granola

ingredients

serves 10

1 spray of vegetable oil spray
225 g/8 oz porridge oats
50 g/1¾ oz desiccated coconut
50 g/1¾ oz flaked almonds
55 g/2 oz linseed meal (ground
    golden linseeds)
¼ tsp salt
125 ml/4 fl oz maple syrup
4 tbsp water
1 tbsp vegetable oil
1 tsp vanilla extract
100 g/3½ oz stoned dried cherries,
    chopped
soya milk, to serve

method

1 Preheat the oven to 140°C/275°F/Gas Mark 1. Line a
large baking tray with baking paper and spray it lightly
with the vegetable oil spray.

2 In a large bowl, combine the oats, coconut, almonds,
linseed meal and salt and stir to mix well. In a small
bowl, combine the maple syrup, water, vegetable oil
and vanilla extract. Pour the liquid mixture over the dry
mixture and stir well. Pour the mixture onto the
prepared baking tray and spread out into an even layer.

3 Bake in the preheated oven for about 45 minutes, then
stir well and spread out again into an even layer.
Continue to bake for a further 30–40 minutes until
crisp and beginning to colour. Stir in the cherries and
leave to cool to room temperature.

4 Store in a tightly covered container for up to a week
at room temperature or serve immediately with
soya milk.

coffee & walnut breakfast muffins

ingredients

makes 12

vegan margarine, for greasing
270 g/9½ oz plain flour
1 tbsp baking powder
2 tbsp espresso powder
1 tsp cinnamon
175 g/6 oz caster sugar
250 ml/9 fl oz soya milk
80 ml/5½ tbsp rapeseed oil
1 tbsp vanilla extract
100 g/3½ oz walnuts, chopped

topping

30 g/1 oz walnuts, finely chopped
15 g/½ oz brown sugar

method

1 Preheat the oven to 180°C/350°F/Gas Mark 4. Lightly grease a muffin tin or place 12 muffin cases in a muffin tin.

2 Sift together the flour, baking powder, espresso powder and cinnamon into a large bowl and stir in the caster sugar.

3 Whisk together the soya milk, oil and vanilla extract in a small bowl. Stir into the dry ingredients adding the chopped walnuts at the same time. Mix until just combined – do not over-mix.

4 Divide the mixture between the holes of the prepared muffin tin and sprinkle the top of each muffin with the finely chopped walnuts and brown sugar. Bake in the preheated oven for 20–25 minutes, or until a skewer inserted into a muffin comes out clean. Allow to cool slightly for 5 minutes before removing from the tin and serving.

sunshine salad with muesli cookies

ingredients
*makes 2 salads and
   30 cookies*

fruit salad
1 large orange
1 grapefruit
1 ruby grapefruit
maple syrup, to taste

cookies
160 g/5¾ oz vegan margarine
300 g/10½ oz granulated sugar
175 g/6 oz plain flour
½ tsp baking powder
40 g/1½ oz linseed meal (ground
   golden linseeds)
1 tsp cinnamon
½ tsp salt
125 ml/4 fl oz soya milk
1 tsp vanilla extract
50 g/1¾ oz raisins
50 g/1¾ oz dates, finely chopped
50 g/1¾ oz walnuts,
   finely chopped
250 g/9 oz porridge oats

method
1 Preheat the oven to 180°C/350°F/Gas Mark 4. Line a
   large baking sheet with baking paper.

2 To make the cookies, cream together the margarine
   and sugar in a large mixing bowl until light and fluffy.
   Sift together the flour and baking powder and stir into
   the bowl with the linseed meal, cinnamon and salt.

3 Whisk together the soya milk and vanilla extract in
   a small bowl and stir into the mixture, adding the
   raisins, dates, walnuts and oats at the same time. Mix
   until thoroughly combined.

4 Roll a little of the cookie mixture into a ball about
   4 cm/1½ inches in diameter. Place on the prepared
   baking sheet and flatten slightly. Continue with the rest
   of the mixture to make about 30 small cookies. Bake in
   the preheated oven for 15 minutes, or until golden.
   Leave to cool on the sheet for 5 minutes before
   transferring to a wire rack to cool completely.

5 To make the salad, use a sharp knife to peel away all the
   skin and pith from the orange and grapefruits. Carefully
   cut v-shaped wedges between each segment of the
   fruit to remove the flesh without the membranes.
   Divide the fruit between two small serving dishes and
   drizzle with maple syrup to taste. Serve each fruit salad
   with two or three cookies (remaining cookies should
   be stored in a container and consumed within 5 days).

tropical porridge

ingredients

serves 2

100 g/3½ oz porridge oats
300 ml/10 fl oz hot water
pinch of salt
50 g/1¾ oz tropical fruit
    and nut mix
1 large or 2 small bananas
reduced-fat coconut milk,
    to serve

method

1 Put the oats into a non-stick saucepan and add the hot water and salt. Stir well and bring to the boil, then reduce the heat and simmer, stirring often, for 5 minutes, until the porridge is thick and fairly smooth.

2 When the porridge is nearly ready, stir in the tropical fruit and nut mix and cook for a further minute.

3 Spoon the porridge into two serving bowls. Peel the banana and slice it over the top. Serve immediately with reduced-fat coconut milk.

herby tofu scramble

ingredients

serves 2

400 g/14 oz firm tofu
12 cherry tomatoes on the vine
olive oil, for roasting
1 small vegan ciabatta loaf
30 g/1 oz vegan margarine
2 garlic cloves, halved and bruised
5 tbsp chopped fresh mixed herbs
     (tarragon, chives, parsley)
salt and pepper
smoked paprika, to taste

method

1 Preheat the oven to 200°C/400°F/Gas Mark 6. If the tofu is packed in water, drain it and press the tofu block between sheets of kitchen paper to remove as much water as possible. Gently crumble the tofu into a large bowl.

2 Place the cherry tomatoes in a medium-sized roasting tin and drizzle lightly with olive oil. Roast in the preheated oven for 5 minutes, or until warm and beginning to split.

3 Cut the ciabatta loaf in half and slice each half lengthways. Toast the bread slices lightly on both sides.

4 Melt the margarine in a large frying pan over a medium heat. Sauté the garlic in the margarine for 1 minute, then remove the garlic from the pan and discard.

5 Put the tofu into the frying pan over a medium heat and fry it in the garlic-infused oil, turning occasionally, for 3–4 minutes, or until just browning. Remove from the heat, stir in the fresh chopped herbs, and add salt and pepper to taste.

6 Sprinkle the tofu scramble with smoked paprika to taste. Serve the scramble immediately on the toasted ciabatta, with the roasted tomatoes on the side.

mushrooms on bruschetta

ingredients

serves 4

12 slices vegan baguette, each
  1 cm/½ inch thick, or 2
  individual vegan baguettes,
  cut lengthways
3 tbsp olive oil
2 garlic cloves, crushed
225 g/8 oz chestnut mushrooms,
  sliced
225 g/8 oz mixed wild mushrooms
2 tsp lemon juice
2 tbsp chopped fresh flat-leaf
  parsley
salt and pepper

method

1 Place the slices of baguette on a ridged griddle pan
  and toast on both sides until golden. Reserve and
  keep warm.

2 Meanwhile, heat the oil in a frying pan. Add the
  garlic and cook gently for a few seconds, then add the
  chestnut mushrooms. Cook, stirring constantly, over a
  high heat for 3 minutes. Add the wild mushrooms and
  cook for a further 2 minutes. Stir in the lemon juice.

3 Season to taste with salt and pepper and stir in the
  chopped parsley.

4 Spoon the mushroom mixture onto the warm toast
  and serve immediately.

bean breakfast burritos

ingredients

serves 2

spicy beans
1 tbsp olive oil
1 onion, finely chopped
1 green pepper, deseeded and
    finely chopped
400 g/14 oz canned aduki beans,
    drained and rinsed
1 tbsp molasses
1 tbsp maple syrup
1 tsp English mustard
½ tsp cinnamon
1 tsp sun-dried tomato purée
400 ml/14 fl oz water
salt and pepper

2 tbsp vegetable oil
2 vegan sausages, defrosted if
    frozen
75 g/2¾ oz pineapple chunks
2 soft vegan tortillas (square ones
    if available)
1 handful fresh baby spinach
    leaves, shredded

method

1 To make the spicy beans, heat the olive oil in a large saucepan over a medium heat and fry the onion and green pepper for 3 minutes, or until softened. Add the remaining ingredients for the spicy beans, bring to the boil then reduce the heat and simmer for 30 minutes. Season to taste with salt and pepper.

2 Heat the vegetable oil in a frying pan over a medium heat. Fry the sausages together with the pineapple chunks for 10 minutes, or until browned. Leave to cool a little and slice the sausages into bite-sized pieces.

3 Divide the bean mixture between the two tortillas and spread to cover the whole surface. Cover the beans with a layer of shredded spinach.

4 Divide the pineapple and sausage pieces between the tortillas, arranging them in a line down the middle if your tortillas are circular, or along one edge if they are square. Roll the tortillas up as tightly as you can to create a spiral effect.

5 Using a serrated knife, slice the tortillas into two or three pieces. Serve immediately.

spinach & sweet potato pancakes

ingredients

serves 4

pancakes

200 ml/7 fl oz soya milk
50 g/1¾ oz plain flour
50 g/1¾ oz chickpea (gram) flour
100 g/3½ oz sweet potato, grated
1 small red onion, finely chopped
vegetable oil, for frying

filling

150 g/5½ oz fresh baby spinach
    leaves, shredded
20 g/¾ oz currants
1 tbsp olive oil
30 g/1 oz pine nuts
salt and pepper

method

1 To make the filling, place the spinach in a saucepan over a medium heat. Add a splash of water and cook for about 2–3 minutes or until wilted. Turn out onto a plate, then blot firmly with kitchen paper to squeeze out as much water as possible. Set aside.

2 To make the pancakes, whisk together the milk, plain flour and chickpea flour in a large bowl. Stir in the sweet potato and onion, and mix thoroughly.

3 Heat a small amount of vegetable oil in a large frying pan over a high heat and pour a quarter of the pancake mixture into the pan, using the back of a spoon to spread the mixture out to the edges of the pan. Fry for 2–3 minutes on each side, turning carefully, until brown and crisp. Transfer to a plate lined with kitchen paper and make three more pancakes.

4 Return the spinach to the saucepan with the currants, olive oil and pine nuts and place over a medium heat. Season with salt and pepper and cook for a minute or until heated through. Take a quarter of the spinach mixture and place on one half of a pancake. Fold over the other half. Repeat with the remaining pancakes.

variation

Use the pancake mixture to make 8–10 mini pancakes and serve as stacks, alternating pancakes with the filling.

raw buckwheat & almond porridge

ingredients

serves 6

almond milk
70 g/2½ oz whole raw almonds,
    soaked overnight in water
300 ml/10 fl oz water

porridge
350 g/12 oz raw buckwheat
    groats, soaked in cold water
    for 90 minutes
1 tsp cinnamon
2 tbsp light agave nectar, plus extra
    to serve
sliced strawberries, to serve

method

1 To make the almond milk, drain the almonds and transfer to a blender or food processor. Blend the almonds with the water. Keep the blender running for a minute or two to break down the almonds as much as possible.

2 Pour the mixture into a sieve lined with muslin and squeeze through as much of the liquid as possible into a large bowl or jug. You should get approximately 300 ml/10 fl oz of raw almond milk.

3 Rinse the soaked buckwheat thoroughly in cold water. Transfer to the blender or food processor with the almond milk, cinnamon and agave nectar. Blend to a slightly coarse texture.

4 Chill the mixture for at least 30 minutes or overnight. It can be stored, covered, in the refrigerator for 3 days.

5 Serve in small bowls, topped with strawberries and agave nectar to taste.

snacks

nutty toffee popcorn

ingredients

serves 2

40 g/1½ oz vegan margarine
40 g/1½ oz brown sugar
1 tbsp golden syrup
70 g/2½ oz cashew nuts
50 g/1¾ oz popping corn
1 tbsp vegetable oil

method

1 Place the margarine, sugar and golden syrup in a saucepan over a medium heat. Bring the temperature up to high and stir continuously for 2 minutes, then remove from the heat and set aside.

2 Toast the cashew nuts in a dry, heavy-based pan over a medium heat for 3–4 minutes, stirring frequently, until they begin to turn golden brown. Remove from the heat and transfer to a plate.

3 In a large, lidded saucepan, stir the popping corn together with the oil until it is well coated. Put the lid on the pan and place over a medium heat. Listen for popping and turn the heat to low. Shake the pan occasionally, holding the lid down firmly. Do not lift the lid until the popping has finished.

4 While the popcorn is still warm, stir in the toasted cashews. Pour over the toffee sauce and stir well to coat the popcorn. Transfer the popcorn to a baking sheet lined with baking paper and allow to cool before serving.

maple-nut granola bars

ingredients

makes 12

1 spray of vegetable oil spray
165 g/5¾ oz porridge oats
50 g/1¾ oz pecan nuts, chopped
50 g/1¾ oz flaked almonds
120 ml/3¾ fl oz maple syrup
50 g/1¾ oz soft light brown sugar
60 g/2¼ oz smooth peanut butter
1 tsp vanilla extract
¼ tsp salt
30 g/1 oz puffed rice cereal
30 g/1 oz linseed meal (ground golden linseeds)

method

1 Preheat the oven to 180°C/350°F/Gas Mark 4. Coat a 23 x 33-cm/9 x 13-inch baking tin with vegetable oil spray.

2 On a large, rimmed baking tray, combine the oats, pecan nuts and almonds and toast in the preheated oven for 5–7 minutes or until lightly browned.

3 Meanwhile, combine the maple syrup, brown sugar and peanut butter in a small saucepan and bring to the boil over a medium heat. Cook, stirring, for about 4–5 minutes or until the mixture thickens slightly. Stir in the vanilla extract and salt.

4 When the oats and nuts are toasted, place them in a mixing bowl and add the rice cereal and linseed meal. Add the syrup mixture to the oat mixture and stir to combine. Spread the syrup-oat mixture into the prepared baking tin and chill in the refrigerator for at least 1 hour before cutting into 12 bars. Store in a tightly covered container at room temperature. Serve at room temperature.

mocha cookies

ingredients

makes 14

115 g/4 oz plain flour
¼ tsp baking powder
15 g/½ oz cocoa powder
125 g/4½ oz brown sugar
1 tbsp espresso powder
125 g/4½ oz vegan margarine
50 g/1¾ oz porridge oats

method

1 Preheat the oven to 180°C/350°F/Gas Mark 4. Line a large baking sheet with baking paper.

2 Sift together the flour, baking powder and cocoa powder in a large mixing bowl. Add the sugar and combine thoroughly.

3 Dissolve the espresso powder in 1 tablespoon of boiling water and stir into the bowl. Add the margarine and oats and mix thoroughly to form a soft dough.

4 Form the mixture into 14 small balls, place on the prepared baking sheet and flatten slightly. Leave spaces between the cookies as they will expand during cooking. Bake in the preheated oven for 15 minutes, or until crisp. Transfer to a wire rack to cool, using a palette knife. Leave to cool completely before serving or storing in an airtight jar for up to 5 days.

lunchbox brownies

ingredients

makes 9

2 tbsp linseed meal (ground golden linseeds)

225 g/8 oz plain flour

¼ tsp bicarbonate of soda

50 g/1¾ oz cocoa powder

275 g/9¾ oz brown sugar

30 g/1 oz vegan dark chocolate

2 tsp vanilla extract

85 g/3 oz vegan margarine, melted, plus extra for greasing

40 g/1½ oz macadamia nuts, roughly chopped

method

1 Preheat the oven to 180°C/350°F/Gas Mark 4. Grease and line a 20-cm/8-inch square baking tin with baking paper.

2 Mix the linseed meal with 3 tablespoons of water and set aside for 10 minutes.

3 Sift together the flour, bicarbonate of soda and cocoa powder in a large bowl. Add the sugar and combine thoroughly.

4 Break the chocolate into small pieces, place in a small bowl and pour over 4 tablespoons of boiling water. Stir thoroughly to melt the chocolate.

5 Stir the linseed paste, melted chocolate, vanilla extract, melted margarine and chopped nuts into the dry ingredients. Use your hands to form the mixture into a soft dough. Press the dough into the prepared baking tin.

6 Bake in the preheated oven for 30 minutes, or until crisp around the edges but the centre is still soft. Carefully lift the brownie out of the tin using the lining paper, leave the paper on and place on a wire rack to cool for 10 minutes. Carefully peel away the paper and cut into nine squares. Leave to cool completely before serving or storing in an airtight tin for up to 5 days.

mango & coconut muffins

ingredients

makes 10

vegan margarine, for greasing
250 g/9 oz plain flour
1 tbsp baking powder
1 tbsp linseed meal (ground golden linseeds)
55 g/2 oz desiccated coconut, plus 2 tbsp for topping
125 g/4½ oz caster sugar
9 cardamom pods
175 ml/6 fl oz soya milk
5 tbsp rapeseed oil
250 g/9 oz fresh, ripe mango, chopped

method

1 Preheat the oven to 190°C/375°F/Gas Mark 5. Lightly grease a muffin tin or place 10 muffin cases in a muffin tin.

2 Sift together the flour and baking powder into a large bowl. Mix in the linseed meal, coconut and sugar.

3 Crush the cardamom pods and remove the seeds. Discard the green pods. Crush the seeds finely in a pestle and mortar or with a rolling pin and stir into the mixture.

4 Whisk together the soya milk and oil in a small bowl and stir into the mixture, adding the mango at the same time. Mix until just combined; do not over-mix.

5 Divide the mixture between the 10 holes of the prepared muffin tin and sprinkle the top of each muffin with a little of the extra coconut. Bake in the preheated oven for 25–30 minutes, or until a skewer inserted into the centre of a muffin comes out clean. Leave to cool for 5 minutes before removing from the tin. Serve or store in a cool place or refrigerator for 2–3 days.

almond cupcakes

ingredients

makes 10

vegan margarine, for greasing
5 tbsp rapeseed oil
4 tbsp plain soya yogurt
160 ml/5½ fl oz soya milk
160 g/5¾ oz caster sugar
3 tbsp almond extract
40 g/1½ oz ground almonds
160 g/5¾ oz plain flour
1½ tsp baking powder
½ tsp salt

icing

60 g/2¼ oz vegan white or milk
    chocolate
100 g/3½ oz icing sugar
1½ tbsp soya milk
toasted flaked almonds,
    to decorate

method

1 Preheat the oven to 180°C/350°F/Gas Mark 4. Lightly grease a cupcake tin or line with 10 paper cases.

2 Place the oil, yogurt, milk, sugar, almond extract and ground almonds in a large mixing bowl. Sift in the flour, baking powder and salt then beat with an electric hand-held whisk until the mixture is well combined.

3 Divide the mixture between the holes of the prepared cupcake tin and bake in the preheated oven for 20–25 minutes, or until well risen and golden. Transfer the cupcakes to a wire rack and leave to cool completely before icing.

4 To make the icing, melt the chocolate in a large heatproof bowl set over a pan of simmering water. Remove from the heat and leave to cool slightly. Beat in the icing sugar and soya milk and spread the icing over the cupcakes with a teaspoon while the icing is still a little warm and easy to spread. Top each cupcake with a few toasted flaked almonds.

guacamole dip

ingredients

serves 4

2 large avocados
juice of 1–2 limes
2 large garlic cloves, crushed
1 tsp mild chilli powder,
    or to taste, plus extra to garnish
salt and pepper

method

1 Cut the avocados in half. Remove the stones and skin and discard.

2 Place the avocado flesh in a food processor with the juice of 1 or 2 limes, according to taste. Add the garlic and chilli powder and process until smooth.

3 Season to taste with salt and pepper. Transfer to a serving bowl, garnish with chilli powder and serve.

raw cashew hummus

ingredients

serves 4

150 g/5½ oz cashew nuts
2 tbsp tahini
juice of 2 lemons
4 tbsp olive oil
½ tsp onion powder
½ tsp garlic powder
sea salt and pepper
paprika and chilli oil, to serve
toasted vegan pitta breads, to serve

method

1 Soak the cashew nuts in a bowl of water for 2 hours.

2 Drain the cashews and place them in a blender or food processor with the tahini, lemon juice, olive oil, onion powder and garlic powder. Process to a smooth paste. Gradually add a little water to adjust the consistency to suit your preference. Taste and adjust the seasoning with salt and pepper.

3 Transfer to a small dish and serve with a dusting of paprika, a drizzle of chilli oil and the toasted pitta breads.

aubergine pâté

ingredients

serves 6

2 large aubergines
4 tbsp extra virgin olive oil
2 garlic cloves, very finely chopped
4 tbsp lemon juice
salt and pepper
2 tbsp roughly chopped fresh
   flat-leaf parsley, to garnish
6 vegan crisp breads, to serve

method

1 Preheat the oven to 180°C/350°F/Gas Mark 4. Score the skins of the aubergines with the point of a sharp knife, without piercing the flesh, and place them on a baking sheet. Bake in the preheated oven for 1¼ hours, or until soft.

2 Remove the aubergines from the oven and leave until cool enough to handle. Cut them in half and, using a spoon, scoop out the flesh into a bowl. Mash the flesh thoroughly.

3 Gradually beat in the olive oil then stir in the garlic and lemon juice. Season to taste with salt and pepper. Cover with clingfilm and store in the refrigerator until required. Garnish with the parsley and serve with crisp breads.

salsa bean dip

ingredients

serves 4

200 g/7 oz cherry tomatoes, quartered

1 small red onion, very finely chopped

200 g/7 oz canned aduki beans, drained and rinsed

½ red pepper, deseeded and finely chopped

½ or 1 red chilli (to taste), deseeded and very finely chopped

2 tsp sun-dried tomato purée

1 tsp agave nectar

large handful of chopped fresh coriander

salt and pepper

chilli oil, to serve

4 small soft vegan tortillas, to serve

method

1 Place the tomatoes, onion, beans, red pepper, chilli, purée, agave nectar and coriander in a large bowl. Mix together well and season to taste with salt and pepper.

2 Cover the bowl and leave in the refrigerator for at least 15 minutes to let the flavours develop. Preheat the grill to medium.

3 Place the tortillas under the preheated grill and lightly toast. Leave to cool slightly then cut into slices.

4 Transfer the bean dip to a small serving bowl. Serve with the sliced tortillas and chilli oil to dip.

crispy courgette crostini

ingredients

serves 6

1 courgette (approx. 200 g/7 oz)
1 tsp salt
½ apple, peeled and grated
1 tbsp chopped fresh mint leaves
2 spring onions, finely chopped
6 slices of vegan French bread
1 garlic clove, halved lengthways
olive oil, to serve
pepper, to serve

method

1 Top and tail the courgette, grate coarsely and spread over a clean, dry tea towel. Sprinkle over the salt and set aside for 5 minutes. Wrap the tea towel around the courgette and squeeze to remove as much moisture as possible.

2 Transfer the courgette to a large mixing bowl and stir in the apple, mint and spring onions.

3 Toast the bread slices lightly on both sides. Rub one side of each slice with the garlic halves.

4 Divide the courgette mixture between the bread slices. Drizzle with a little olive oil and grind a little pepper over them before serving.

sweet potato chips

ingredients

serves 4

2 sprays of vegetable oil spray
900 g/2 lb sweet potatoes
½ tsp salt
½ tsp ground cumin
¼ tsp cayenne pepper

method

1 Preheat the oven to 230°C/450°F/Gas Mark 8. Spray a large baking tray with vegetable oil spray.

2 Peel the sweet potatoes and slice into 5-mm/¼-inch thick spears about 7.5 cm/3 inches long. Spread the sweet potatoes on the prepared baking tray and spray them with vegetable oil spray.

3 In a small bowl, combine the salt, cumin and cayenne pepper. Sprinkle the spice mixture evenly over the sweet potatoes and then toss to coat.

4 Spread the sweet potatoes out into a single layer and bake in the preheated oven for about 15–20 minutes or until cooked through and lightly coloured. Serve hot.

nachos with salsa & raita

ingredients

serves 4

200 g/7 oz vegan lightly salted
    tortilla chips

salsa verde

2 garlic cloves
1 tbsp wholegrain mustard
2 tbsp capers
4 tbsp chopped fresh flat-leaf
    parsley
2 tbsp chopped fresh mint leaves
2 tbsp chopped fresh basil leaves
150 ml/5 fl oz olive oil
1 tbsp fresh lemon juice
salt and pepper

cucumber raita

1 tsp cumin seeds
150 ml/5 fl oz plain soya yogurt
85 g/3 oz cucumber, peeled and
    grated
40 g/1½ oz unpeeled cucumber,
    finely chopped
¼ tsp cayenne pepper

method

1 To make the salsa verde, place the garlic, mustard,
    capers, chopped herbs, 50 ml/2 fl oz of the olive oil and
    the lemon juice into a food processor. Process until the
    mixture is finely chopped. While keeping the machine
    running, gradually drizzle in the remaining olive oil.
    Season to taste with salt and pepper. Chill for at least
    30 minutes in the refrigerator before serving.

2 To make the raita, dry roast the cumin seeds in a dry,
    heavy-based frying pan over a high heat. Shake
    constantly for a minute or two, or until lightly toasted.
    Tip out the seeds from the pan and crush them with a
    pestle and mortar or rolling pin. Place the yogurt,
    grated cucumber, chopped cucumber and cayenne
    pepper in a large bowl, then add the toasted crushed
    cumin seeds. Stir until thoroughly mixed. Chill for at
    least 30 minutes in the refrigerator before serving.

3 Serve the dips in small bowls with the tortilla chips on
    a large serving plate.

vegetable pakoras

ingredients

serves 4

6 tbsp chickpea (gram) flour
½ tsp salt
1 tsp chilli powder
1 tsp baking powder
1½ tsp white cumin seeds
1 tsp pomegranate seeds
300 ml/10 fl oz water
¼ bunch of fresh coriander,
    finely chopped, plus extra
    sprigs to garnish
vegetables of your choice, such as:
    cauliflower, cut into small
    florets; onions, cut into rings;
    potatoes, sliced; aubergines,
    sliced; or fresh spinach leaves
vegetable oil, for deep-frying

method

1 Sift the gram flour into a large bowl. Add the salt, chilli powder, baking powder, cumin and pomegranate seeds and blend together well. Pour in the water and beat well to form a smooth batter. Add the chopped coriander and mix well, then set aside.

2 Dip the prepared vegetables into the batter, carefully shaking off any excess.

3 Heat enough oil for deep-frying in a wok, deep-fat fryer or a large, heavy-based saucepan until it reaches 180°C/350°F, or until a cube of bread browns in 30 seconds. Using tongs, place the battered vegetables in the oil and deep-fry, in batches, turning once.

4 Repeat this process until all of the batter has been used up. Transfer the battered vegetables to crumpled kitchen paper and drain thoroughly. Garnish with coriander sprigs and serve immediately.

lunch

gazpacho soup

ingredients

serves 6

600 g/1 lb 5 oz fresh ripe tomatoes
10 sun-dried tomatoes in oil
½ red onion, chopped
2 garlic cloves
1 large handful fresh basil leaves
2 tbsp olive oil
1 tsp vegan stock powder
2 tbsp red wine vinegar
1 red pepper, deseeded and finely
    chopped
½ cucumber, peeled and finely
    chopped
150 g/5½ oz ice cubes
salt and pepper

method

1 Place the fresh tomatoes, sun-dried tomatoes, onion, garlic, basil, olive oil, stock powder and vinegar into a food processor or blender and process until smooth. Season to taste with salt and pepper.

2 Transfer to a large bowl and stir in the red pepper, cucumber and ice cubes. Chill thoroughly in the refrigerator before stirring well, check the seasoning again and serve in small bowls.

spicy courgette & rice soup

ingredients

serves 4

2 tbsp vegetable oil

4 garlic cloves, thinly sliced

1 tbsp mild red chilli powder, or
    to taste

¼–½ tsp ground cumin

1.5 litres/2¾ pints vegan stock

2 courgettes, cut into bite-sized
    chunks

4 tbsp long-grain rice

salt and pepper

fresh oregano sprigs, to garnish

lime wedges, to serve

method

1 Heat the oil in a heavy-based saucepan over a medium heat. Add the garlic and cook for 2 minutes, or until softened. Add the chilli powder and cumin and cook over a medium–low heat for 1 minute.

2 Stir in the stock, courgettes and rice, then cook over a medium–high heat for 10 minutes, or until the courgettes are just tender and the rice is cooked through. Season to taste with salt and pepper.

3 Ladle into warmed bowls, garnish with oregano sprigs and serve immediately with lime wedges.

corn chowder

ingredients

serves 6

1 tbsp olive oil
1 onion, finely chopped
1 carrot, finely chopped
1 leek, finely chopped
2 garlic cloves, finely chopped
1 tsp dried thyme
1 tbsp plain flour
1.5 litres/2¾ pints vegan stock
200 g/7 oz sweet potatoes,
    finely chopped
500 g/1 lb 2 oz frozen sweetcorn
    kernels
salt and pepper

method

1 Heat the oil in a large frying pan over a low heat. Gently fry the onion, carrot, leek, garlic and thyme for 5–8 minutes, or until the onion is softened and translucent.

2 Stir in the flour and cook for a further minute, then pour in the stock and stir well.

3 Add the sweet potato to the pan, bring to the boil and then reduce the heat. Simmer for 20 minutes, stirring frequently, until the sweet potato is soft.

4 Stir in the sweetcorn kernels and cook for a further 5 minutes.

5 Transfer 500 ml/18 fl oz of the chowder to a food processor or blender. Blend until smooth and then return to the pan. Mix thoroughly and season to taste with salt and pepper. Reheat the soup then serve immediately.

sweet potato soup

ingredients

serves 6

2 tsp vegetable oil
1 onion, diced
1 tbsp finely chopped fresh ginger
1 tbsp vegan Thai red curry paste
1 tsp salt
660 g /1 lb 7 oz sweet potatoes,
    diced
400 ml/14 fl oz canned
    reduced-fat coconut milk
1 litre/1¾ pints vegan stock
juice of 1 lime
30 g/1 oz finely chopped fresh
    coriander, to garnish

method

1 In a large, heavy-based saucepan, heat the oil over a medium–high heat. Add the onion and ginger and cook, stirring, for about 5 minutes or until soft. Add the curry paste and salt and cook, stirring, for a further minute or so. Add the sweet potatoes, coconut milk and stock and bring to the boil. Reduce the heat to medium and simmer, uncovered, for about 20 minutes or until the sweet potatoes are soft.

2 Purée the soup, either in batches in a blender or food processor or using a hand-held blender. Return the soup to the heat and bring back up to a simmer. Just before serving, stir in the lime juice. Serve hot, garnished with coriander.

thai vermicelli soup

ingredients

serves 4

15 g/½ oz dried shiitake
    mushrooms
1.2 litres/2 pints vegan stock
1 tbsp groundnut oil
4 spring onions, sliced
115 g/4 oz baby corn, sliced
2 garlic cloves, crushed
2 fresh kaffir lime leaves, chopped
2 tbsp vegan Thai red curry paste
85 g/3 oz rice vermicelli noodles
1 tbsp light soy sauce
2 tbsp chopped fresh coriander,
    to garnish

method

1 Place the mushrooms in a bowl, cover with the stock and leave to soak for 20 minutes.

2 Heat the groundnut oil in a saucepan over a medium heat. Add the spring onions, baby corn, garlic and kaffir lime leaves. Fry for 3 minutes to soften.

3 Add the red curry paste, soaked mushrooms and their soaking liquid. Bring to the boil and simmer for 5 minutes, stirring occasionally.

4 Add the noodles and soy sauce to the red curry mixture in the pan. Return the pan to the boil and simmer for a further 4 minutes until the noodles are just cooked. Ladle into warmed bowls, garnish with the chopped coriander and serve immediately.

maple-glazed tofu salad

ingredients

serves 4

400 g/14 oz firm tofu
1 tbsp olive oil
125 ml/4 fl oz pineapple juice
125 ml/4 fl oz maple syrup
1 tbsp soy sauce
2 tbsp wholegrain mustard
mixed salad leaves, to serve

method

1 Drain the tofu and press with kitchen paper to remove excess water. Cut into eight slices, approximately 1 cm/½ inch thick.

2 Heat the oil in a large, heavy-based frying pan over a medium heat. Fry the tofu on both sides for 5–8 minutes, turning gently, or until golden.

3 Meanwhile, put the pineapple juice, maple syrup, soy sauce and mustard in a bowl and stir thoroughly to combine. Pour the mixture over the tofu in the pan and reduce the heat to a simmer. Cook for 20 minutes, turning the tofu once.

4 Serve the tofu slices warm or cold, on a bed of mixed salad leaves.

avocado & grapefruit salad

ingredients

serves 2

1 ruby grapefruit, broken into
    segments
2 avocados, sliced
½ red onion, finely sliced
50 g/1¾ oz mixed salad leaves

dressing

4 dried dates, finely chopped
1 tbsp olive oil
1 tbsp walnut oil
1 tbsp white wine vinegar

method

1 To make the dressing, combine the finely chopped
   dates with the olive oil, walnut oil and white wine
   vinegar in a small bowl, using a fork.

2 Place the grapefruit segments, avocado slices and
   onion slices on a bed of fresh salad leaves in a large
   salad bowl. Pour the dressing over the salad and toss,
   using two forks, to mix thoroughly. Serve immediately.

chickpea & quinoa salad

ingredients

serves 4

50 g/1¾ oz red quinoa
1 red chilli, deseeded and finely
    chopped
8 spring onions, chopped
3 tbsp finely chopped fresh mint
2 tbsp olive oil
2 tbsp fresh lemon juice
30 g/1 oz chickpea (gram) flour
1 tsp ground cumin
½ tsp paprika
1 tbsp vegetable oil
150 g/5½ oz canned chickpeas,
    drained and rinsed

method

1 Place the quinoa in a medium saucepan and then cover with boiling water. Place over a low heat and simmer for 10 minutes, or until just cooked. Drain and refresh with cold water, drain again. Transfer to a large bowl and toss together with the red chilli, spring onion and mint to mix thoroughly.

2 Combine the olive oil and lemon juice in a small bowl using a fork.

3 Sift the chickpea flour, cumin and paprika together into a wide, deep bowl. Place the vegetable oil in a medium frying pan over a medium heat. Roll the chickpeas in the spiced flour then fry gently in the pan, stirring frequently, for 2–3 minutes, allowing the chickpeas to brown in patches.

4 Stir the warm chickpeas into the quinoa mixture and quickly stir in the lemon-oil dressing. Serve warm or chilled.

crunchy thai-style salad

ingredients

serves 4

1 slightly under ripe mango
5 Romaine or Cos lettuce leaves, torn into pieces
100 g/3½ oz beansprouts
handful of fresh coriander leaves
25 g/1 oz roasted unsalted peanuts, crushed

dressing

juice of 1 lime
2 tbsp light soy sauce
1 tsp soft light brown sugar
1 shallot, very thinly sliced
1 garlic clove, finely chopped
1 red bird's eye chilli, deseeded and very thinly sliced
1 tbsp chopped fresh mint

method

1 To make the dressing, mix the lime juice, soy sauce and sugar together in a bowl then stir in the shallot, garlic, chilli and mint.

2 Peel the mango using a sharp knife or potato peeler. Slice the flesh from either side and around the stone. Thinly slice or shred the flesh.

3 Place the torn lettuce, beansprouts, coriander leaves and mango in a serving bowl. Gently toss together. Spoon the dressing over the top, scatter with the peanuts and serve immediately.

bean & wild rice salad

ingredients

serves 6

175 g/6 oz wild rice
200 g/7 oz canned kidney beans,
    drained and rinsed
200 g/7 oz canned flageolet beans,
    drained and rinsed
200 g/7 oz canned haricot beans,
    drained and rinsed
1 red onion, thinly sliced
4 spring onions, finely chopped
1 garlic clove, crushed

dressing

4 tbsp olive oil
2 tbsp balsamic vinegar
1 tsp dried oregano

method

1 Place the rice in a large saucepan, cover with water and bring to the boil. Reduce the heat then simmer for 45 minutes, or according to the packet instructions, until the rice is just tender and beginning to 'pop'. If necessary, add more boiling water as the rice cooks. When the rice is cooked, drain, refresh with cold water and drain again.

2 To make the dressing, combine all the ingredients in a small bowl with a fork or small whisk.

3 Place all the beans in a large salad bowl with the onion, spring onion and garlic. Add the cooled rice and pour in the dressing. Mix together thoroughly, using a wooden or metal spoon. Chill in the refrigerator before serving.

couscous with roast tomatoes

ingredients

serves 6

300 g/10½ oz cherry tomatoes
3 tbsp olive oil
125 g/4½ oz couscous
200 ml/7 fl oz boiling water
30 g/1 oz pine nuts, toasted
5 tbsp roughly chopped mint
finely grated zest of 1 lemon
½ tbsp lemon juice
salt and pepper

method

1 Preheat the oven to 220°C/425°F/Gas Mark 7. Place the tomatoes and 1 tablespoon of the oil in an ovenproof dish. Toss together, then roast for 7–8 minutes in the preheated oven until the tomatoes are soft and the skins have burst. Leave to stand for 5 minutes.

2 Put the couscous in a heatproof bowl. Pour over the boiling water, cover and leave to stand for 8–10 minutes until soft and the liquid is absorbed. Fluff up with a fork.

3 Add the tomatoes and their juices, the pine nuts, mint, lemon zest, lemon juice and the remaining oil to the couscous. Season with salt and pepper, then gently toss together. Serve warm or cold.

ginger vegetable tempura

ingredients

serves 6

1.5 litres/2¾ pints vegetable oil, for deep-frying
600 g/1 lb 5 oz fresh seasonal vegetables, cut into large pieces (such as peppers, mangetout, asparagus, broccoli, aubergines, courgettes)
1 tbsp golden syrup or maple syrup, to serve
1 tbsp paprika, to serve

ginger batter

250 g/9 oz plain flour
250 g/9 oz cornflour
300 ml/10 fl oz soda water
300 ml/10 fl oz sparkling vegan ginger beer

method

1 Preheat the oven to 160°C/325°F/Gas Mark 3.

2 To make the ginger batter, place the flour and cornflour in a large, wide bowl. Slowly pour in the soda water and ginger beer, stirring quickly to create a smooth batter. If there are any lumps, stir again to remove.

3 Heat the oil in a large saucepan or wok over a high heat, until a drop of batter floats quickly to the top and sizzles. Dip each piece of vegetable in the batter, shake off the excess and deep-fry for about 5 minutes, or until crisp and beginning to brown. Fry the vegetables in small batches, drain on kitchen paper and keep on an ovenproof plate in the preheated oven while you finish the frying. Scoop out any stray pieces of batter from the oil between batches so that they do not burn and taint the oil.

4 Serve the vegetables piled on a large serving plate, drizzled with the syrup and lightly dusted with paprika.

layered tomato, pepper & basil

ingredients

serves 4

1 tsp olive oil

2 shallots, finely chopped

2 garlic cloves, crushed

2 red peppers, peeled, deseeded
  and sliced into strips

1 orange pepper, peeled, deseeded
  and sliced into strips

4 tomatoes, thinly sliced

2 tbsp shredded fresh basil,
  plus extra leaves to garnish

pepper

method

1 Lightly brush four ramekin dishes with the oil. Mix the shallots and garlic together in a bowl and season with pepper to taste.

2 Layer the red and orange peppers with the tomatoes in the prepared ramekin dishes, sprinkling each layer with the shallot mixture and shredded basil. When all the ingredients have been added, cover lightly with clingfilm or baking paper. Weigh down using small weights and leave in the refrigerator for at least 6 hours, or preferably overnight.

3 When ready to serve, remove the weights and carefully run a knife around the edges. Invert onto serving plates and serve garnished with basil leaves.

walnut pâté on ciabatta

ingredients

serves 4

walnut pâté

125 g/4½ oz walnuts, roughly
 chopped
125 g/4½ oz fresh brown vegan
 breadcrumbs
1 small red onion, chopped
1 tbsp chopped fresh tarragon
1 tbsp chopped fresh chives
1 tsp tomato purée
1 tsp soy sauce
1 tbsp vegan red wine (optional)
2 tsp walnut oil, plus extra as
 needed

salt and pepper
vegan ciabatta loaf, sliced,
 or crackers

method

1 Place all the pâté ingredients in a large bowl and mix
 together well with a wooden spoon. Season to taste
 with salt and pepper. Transfer to a food processor and
 blend until it forms a smooth paste. If the breadcrumbs
 are quite dry, you may need to add a little more oil or
 red wine, if using.

2 Transfer the mixture to four small pots and chill in the
 refrigerator before serving. Serve the pâté with the
 slices of ciabatta or crackers.

smoked tofu & vegetable baguette

ingredients

serves 2–4

1 small courgette, sliced
1 red or yellow pepper, deseeded
    and sliced
1 red onion, cut into 8 pieces
2 tbsp olive oil
35-cm/14-inch vegan baguette
1 handful of fresh basil, chopped
1 handful of fresh rocket, chopped
70 g/2½ oz smoked tofu, sliced
70 g/2½ oz tomatoes, sliced
1 tbsp balsamic vinegar

tapenade

12 black olives, stoned and roughly
    chopped
1 garlic clove
1 tbsp olive oil
salt and pepper

method

1 Preheat the oven to 190°C/375°F/Gas Mark 5. Place the courgette, pepper and red onion on a baking sheet, drizzle over the olive oil and toss together so that the vegetables are coated with the oil. Roast in the preheated oven for 25 minutes, or until softened and beginning to brown.

2 To make the tapenade, place the olives, garlic and oil in a food processor and process to a rough paste. Season to taste with salt and pepper.

3 Cut the baguette in half lengthways and spread the cut side of the top half with the tapenade.

4 On the cut side of the bottom half, layer the roast vegetables, including their oil, the basil and rocket, then the tofu and tomatoes and finally drizzle over the balsamic vinegar – the fillings will be piled high. Place the tapenade half on top and press down firmly to compress the filling.

5 Wrap the baguette very tightly in clingfilm or kitchen foil and refrigerate for at least an hour before serving. Slice carefully with a serrated knife into portions.

mediterranean wrap

ingredients

serves 4

1 small courgette, thickly sliced
1 red or yellow pepper, deseeded and roughly chopped
1 tbsp olive oil
4 soft vegan flatbreads
6 tbsp sun-dried tomato purée
85 g/3 oz fresh baby spinach leaves
4 artichoke hearts in oil, quartered
8 sun-dried tomatoes in oil, quartered
16 black olives, stoned and halved
1 handful of fresh basil leaves, torn

method

1 Preheat the oven to 190°C/375°F/Gas Mark 5. Place the courgette and pepper on a baking sheet, pour over the oil and toss together so that the vegetables are well coated. Roast the vegetables in the preheated oven for 20 minutes, or until softened and beginning to brown. Remove from the oven.

2 Spread each flatbread with a thin layer of sun-dried tomato purée. Shred the spinach and divide it between the flatbreads.

3 Mix the roast vegetables together with the artichoke hearts, sun-dried tomatoes, olives and basil in a large bowl. Divide the mixture between the flatbreads, spreading the filling evenly on top of the shredded spinach. Roll the flatbreads up tightly, slice in half and serve immediately.

mushroom & pesto panini

ingredients

serves 2

25 g/1 oz vegan margarine
200 g/7 oz button mushrooms, sliced
1 onion, sliced
large handful of fresh flat-leaf parsley, chopped
1 vegan ciabatta loaf
olive oil, for brushing
salt and pepper

pesto

55 g/2 oz cashew nuts
35 g/1¼ oz fresh basil leaves
2 garlic cloves, crushed
4 tbsp olive or hemp oil
salt and pepper

method

1 To make the pesto, lightly toast the cashew nuts in a dry, heavy-based pan until they begin to brown.

2 Place the toasted cashews, basil, garlic, oil and salt and pepper to taste into a food processor and pulse to a rough paste. Alternatively, chop the cashews and basil finely and use a pestle and mortar to grind all the pesto ingredients to a paste.

3 Melt the margarine in a frying pan over a low heat and gently fry the mushrooms, onion and chopped parsley for 5 minutes, or until the onion is soft. Season to taste with salt and pepper.

4 Slice the ciabatta loaf lengthways and then slice each piece in half widthways. Lightly brush the outsides of the bread slices with olive oil.

5 Divide the pesto into four portions and spread onto the cut side of each bread slice. Divide the warm mushroom mixture between two bread slices then sandwich with the other two slices.

6 Heat a dry griddle pan and cook the sandwiches for 2–3 minutes on each side, pressing down firmly to flatten them and produce griddled stripes.

lunchtime bean burgers

ingredients

serves 4

1 tbsp sunflower oil,
    plus extra for brushing
1 onion, finely chopped
1 garlic clove, finely chopped
1 tsp ground coriander
1 tsp ground cumin
115 g/4 oz white mushrooms,
    finely chopped
425 g/15 oz canned borlotti or red
    kidney beans, drained
    and rinsed
2 tbsp chopped fresh flat-leaf
    parsley
plain flour, for dusting
salt and pepper
vegan hamburger rolls and salad,
    to serve

method

1 Heat the oil in a heavy-based frying pan over a medium heat. Add the onion and cook, stirring frequently, for 5 minutes, or until softened. Add the garlic, coriander and cumin and cook, stirring, for a further minute. Add the mushrooms and cook, stirring frequently, for 4–5 minutes until all the liquid has evaporated. Transfer to a bowl.

2 Put the beans in a small bowl and mash with a fork. Stir into the mushroom mixture with the parsley and season with salt and pepper.

3 Preheat the grill to medium–high. Divide the mixture equally into four portions, dust lightly with flour and shape into flat, round burgers. Brush with oil and cook under the grill for 4–5 minutes on each side. Serve in hamburger buns with salad.

easy vegetable sushi

ingredients

serves 4–6

200 g/7 oz sushi rice
2–3 tbsp Japanese rice vinegar
pinch of salt
1 tbsp Japanese sweet rice wine
    (mirin)
7 sheets Japanese sushi nori,
    pretoasted
½ cucumber, cut into matchsticks
1 red pepper, deseeded and cut
    into matchsticks
1 avocado, cut into matchsticks
4 spring onions, halved lengthwise
soy sauce, wasabi paste and
    pickled ginger, to serve
    (optional)

method

1 Place the rice in a medium saucepan and cover with 375 ml/13 fl oz of water. Bring to the boil, then reduce the heat to low, cover and leave to cook for 20 minutes. When cooked, drain the rice and transfer to a large bowl. Gently fold in the rice vinegar, salt and mirin and leave to cool.

2 When the rice is cold, place one sheet of pretoasted nori onto a sushi rolling mat, shiny side down, and spread a thin layer of rice all over, leaving a 1-cm/ ½-inch border along the far edge. Add a selection of the vegetable pieces, arranged in lines running the same way as the bamboo of the mat.

3 Use the mat to carefully lift the edge of the nori closest to you, roll it away from you and tuck it in as tightly as you can. Continue to roll the nori up tightly and, if necessary, moisten the far edge with a little water to seal the roll together. Repeat with the remaining nori sheets, rice and vegetables. Chill in the refrigerator, wrapped tightly in clingfilm, until required. (It is possible to do this step without a sushi mat, if you do not have one.)

4 To serve, cut each roll into slices about 2.5 cm/1 inch thick. Serve with soy sauce and wasabi paste for dipping and pickled ginger as an accompaniment, if desired.

stuffed potato skins

ingredients

serves 2

vegetable oil, for greasing
2 equal-sized baking potatoes
olive oil, for roasting and frying
3 vegan bacon-style rashers
1 tbsp chopped fresh mixed herbs,
     such as sage, parsley, oregano
10 g/¼ oz vegan margarine
salt and pepper

method

1 Preheat the oven to 190°C/375°F/Gas Mark 5. Lightly grease a baking sheet.

2 Score a ring around each potato, in the place where you will eventually cut them in half. Wrap them in kitchen paper and microwave for 6–10 minutes, or until cooked through. Unwrap and leave until cool enough to handle. Cut the potatoes in half and carefully scoop out the flesh, leaving a skin around 1 cm/½ inch thick. Set the flesh aside in a medium bowl.

3 Rub the outside of the potato skins with olive oil and place them, cut-side down, on the prepared baking sheet. Bake in the preheated oven for 15 minutes, or until browned, then remove from the oven and transfer to a clean baking sheet, cut-side up.

4 Heat some olive oil in a frying pan over a medium heat. Fry the rashers for 5 minutes, or until crisp, and then chop finely or crumble them. Mash the reserved potato flesh with a fork, and then mix in the rashers and chopped herbs. Season to taste with salt and pepper.

5 Preheat the grill to high. Pile the mashed potato back into the potato skins, make ridges on top with a fork and dot with a little vegan margarine. Place under the hot grill for 5 minutes until the tops are golden and crisp. Serve immediately.

thai tofu cakes with chilli dip

ingredients

serves 4

300 g/10½ oz firm tofu, drained weight, coarsely grated
1 lemon grass stalk, finely chopped
2 garlic cloves, chopped
2.5-cm/1-inch piece fresh ginger, peeled and grated
2 kaffir lime leaves, finely chopped (optional)
2 shallots, finely chopped
2 fresh red chillies, deseeded and finely chopped
4 tbsp chopped fresh coriander
90 g/3¼ oz plain flour, plus extra for dusting
½ tsp salt
corn oil, for cooking

chilli dip

3 tbsp white distilled vinegar
2 spring onions, finely sliced
1 tbsp caster sugar
2 fresh red chillies, deseeded and chopped
2 tbsp chopped fresh coriander
pinch of salt

method

1 To make the chilli dip, mix all the ingredients together in a small serving bowl and set aside.

2 Mix the tofu with the lemon grass, garlic, ginger, lime leaves, if using, shallots, chillies and coriander in a mixing bowl. Stir in the flour and salt to make a coarse, sticky paste. Cover and chill in the refrigerator for 1 hour to let the mixture firm up slightly.

3 Form the mixture into eight large walnut-sized balls and, using floured hands, flatten into circles. Heat enough oil to cover the bottom of a large, heavy-based frying pan over a medium heat. Cook the cakes in two batches, turning halfway through, for 4–6 minutes, or until golden brown. Drain on kitchen paper and serve warm with the chilli dip.

variation

If you prefer a milder dip, omit the chillies and flavour with Chinese five spice instead.

roast vegetable pizza

ingredients
makes two pizzas

1 green pepper, sliced
1 red or yellow pepper, sliced
1 courgette, sliced
½ small aubergine, sliced
1 red onion, sliced
2 tbsp olive oil, plus extra for the
    sauce, base and greasing
1 handful of fresh basil leaves, torn
1 handful of black olives, halved
1 tbsp pine nuts

tomato sauce
1 onion, finely chopped
2 garlic cloves, crushed
400 g/14 oz chopped tomatoes
1 tsp brown sugar
1 tsp sun-dried tomato purée
1 tsp dried oregano
salt and pepper

pizza base
375 g/13 oz strong white flour,
    plus extra for dusting
1 tbsp caster sugar
7 g/¼ oz easy-blend dried yeast

method
1 Preheat the oven to 200°C/400°F/Gas Mark 6. Lightly grease two baking sheets. Put the peppers, courgette, aubergine and red onion into a large bowl with the olive oil and mix well until coated with oil. Transfer to a roasting tin and roast for 30 minutes, or until just starting to brown. Remove from the oven and set aside.

2 To make the sauce, heat 1 tbsp of oil in a large frying pan. Fry the onion for 4–5 minutes, then add the garlic and cook for a further minute. Stir in the tomatoes, sugar, purée and oregano. Simmer gently for 6–8 minutes, until very thick. Season to taste with salt and pepper then remove from the heat and leave to cool.

3 To make the pizza base, sift together the flour, 1 tsp of salt, the sugar and yeast in a large bowl. Stir in 2 tbsp of oil and 225 ml/8 fl oz of warm water. Turn the mixture out onto a floured surface and knead for 8–10 minutes. Roll into two 25-cm/10-inch rounds and place on the two prepared sheets. Mix the basil into the sauce and spread evenly over the bases. Top with the olives, vegetables and pine nuts. Leave to rise in a warm place for 20 minutes. Increase the oven to 230°C/450°F/Gas Mark 8. Bake for 10–12 minutes, or until golden brown. Leave to cool for 5 minutes then serve.

spicy black bean tacos

ingredients

serves 4

2 tbsp olive oil
1 onion, thinly sliced
2 garlic cloves, finely chopped
1 green pepper, deseeded and
    sliced
2 tbsp sun-dried tomato purée
2 tbsp chipotle chilli paste (or other
    chilli paste)
800 g/1 lb 12 oz canned black
    beans, drained and rinsed
100 g/3½ oz tomatoes, roughly
    chopped
8 vegan taco shells
150 g/5½ oz iceberg lettuce,
    shredded
1 avocado, sliced

method

1 Preheat the oven to 180°C/350°F/Gas Mark 4.

2 Heat the oil in a large frying pan over a medium heat.
   Fry the onion, garlic and green pepper for 5 minutes,
   or until the onion is softened and translucent. Stir in
   the tomato purée, chilli paste and black beans and
   cook for a further 5 minutes. Stir in the chopped
   tomatoes and immediately remove from the heat.

3 Place the taco shells upside down on a baking sheet
   and warm in the preheated oven for 3 minutes.

4 Mix the lettuce and avocado together in a small bowl.
   Divide the mixture between the taco shells. Reheat the
   bean mixture if necessary and divide the mixture
   between the warmed tacos. Serve immediately.

quick ginger & miso stir-fry

ingredients

serves 2

sauce

1 tsp miso paste dissolved in 2 tbsp
  boiling water

1 tbsp tomato purée

2.5-cm/1-inch piece fresh ginger,
  peeled

2 tbsp vegetable oil

1 tbsp sesame oil

1 green pepper, deseeded and cut
  into matchsticks

1 red pepper, deseeded and cut
  into matchsticks

¼ white cabbage, cored and thinly
  sliced

1 carrot, cut into matchsticks

1 red chilli, deseeded and finely
  chopped

6 spring onions, finely chopped

50 g/1¾ oz green soya (edamame)
  beans

50 g/1¾ oz cashew nuts, roughly
  chopped

cooked rice or vegan noodles,
  to serve

method

1 To make the sauce, mix together the warm miso and
  the tomato purée in a small bowl. Grate the ginger
  coarsely, then gather up the grated ginger and
  squeeze the juice into the miso mixture.

2 Heat the vegetable oil and sesame oil together in
  a large wok over a high heat. Stir-fry the peppers,
  cabbage, carrot, chilli, onions, soya beans and
  nuts for 5 minutes.

3 Stir in the miso-ginger sauce and cook for a further
  minute.

4 Serve immediately, with rice or noodles.

cornbread with spicy potatoes

ingredients

serves 6

spicy potatoes
450 g/1 lb potatoes, chopped in small pieces
2 tbsp olive oil, plus extra for greasing
1 large onion, sliced
1 tsp dried thyme
¼ tsp turmeric
¼ tsp smoked paprika
¼ tsp salt

cornbread
500 ml/18 fl oz soya milk
2 tsp cider vinegar
325 g/11½ oz cornmeal
140 g/5 oz plain flour
2 tsp baking powder
½ tsp salt
80 ml/5½ tbsp rapeseed oil
2 tbsp maple syrup

chilli oil, to serve

method

1 To make the spicy potatoes, place the chopped potato in a medium saucepan of water over a high heat. Boil for 10–15 minutes, or until cooked through, and drain. Heat the oil in a large frying pan and fry the potatoes, onion, thyme, spices and salt for 8–10 minutes, or until golden.

2 Preheat the oven to 180°C/350°F/Gas Mark 4. Grease a 20-cm/8-inch round springform baking tin.

3 To make the cornbread, whisk together the soya milk and the vinegar in a medium bowl, and leave to stand for 5 minutes. In a large bowl, sift together the cornmeal, flour, baking powder and salt.

4 Whisk the oil and maple syrup into the milk mixture and then pour into the dry ingredients. Mix the batter together thoroughly and spoon into the prepared baking tin.

5 Bake in the preheated oven for 25–30 minutes, or until lightly golden, and leave to cool for 5 minutes. Turn out onto a serving dish and top with the spiced potatoes, reheating them if necessary. Top with a drizzle of chilli oil before serving.

dinner

mushroom & spinach calzones

ingredients

makes 2 large calzones

dough

375 g/13 oz plain flour,
   plus extra for dusting
1 tsp salt
1 tbsp caster sugar
7 g/¼ oz easy-blend dried yeast
2 tbsp olive oil
225 ml/8 fl oz warm water

filling

2 tbsp olive oil
2 onions, sliced
3 garlic cloves, finely chopped
200 g/7 oz mixed mushrooms,
   roughly chopped
2 tbsp pine nuts
2 tbsp vegan dry white wine
1 tbsp chopped fresh basil leaves
175 g/6 oz fresh baby spinach
   leaves, shredded
salt and pepper

salad leaves and sliced tomatoes,
   to serve

method

1 Preheat the oven to 190°C/375°F/Gas Mark 5. Flour a
large baking sheet.

2 To make the filling, heat the oil in a large saucepan
over a medium heat. Fry the onions, garlic and
mushrooms until the onions are soft and translucent.
Stir in the pine nuts and the wine and cook for a further
2 minutes. Stir in the basil and spinach and cook for a
further 2 minutes until the spinach is just wilted.
Season to taste with salt and pepper.

3 To make the dough, mix together the flour, salt, sugar
and yeast in a large bowl. Stir in the oil and water. Turn
the mixture onto a floured board and knead for
10 minutes until smooth. Roll the dough into
two 26-cm/10½-inch circles.

4 Divide the filling between the dough circles, placing
it on one half of the circle and leaving a margin of
4 cm/1½ inches around the edge. Fold the uncovered
side of the dough over the filling and flatten the edges
together, then use your fingers or a fork to fold and
crimp the edges together.

5 Transfer the calzones to the prepared baking sheet and
bake in the preheated oven for 15–20 minutes, or until
beginning to brown. Serve with salad and tomatoes.

aubergine & chickpea penne

ingredients

serves 4

large pinch of saffron threads
450 ml/16 fl oz vegan stock
2 tbsp olive oil
1 large onion, roughly chopped
1 tsp cumin seeds, crushed
350 g/12 oz aubergine, diced
1 large red pepper, deseeded and
    chopped
400 g/14 oz canned chopped
    tomatoes with garlic
1 tsp ground cinnamon
30 g/1 oz fresh coriander, leaves
    and stalks separated and
    roughly chopped
400 g/14 oz canned chickpeas,
    drained and rinsed
280 g/10 oz vegan dried penne
salt and pepper
harissa or chilli sauce, to serve

method

1 Toast the saffron threads in a dry frying pan set over a medium heat for 20–30 seconds, just until they begin to give off their aroma. Place in a small bowl and crumble with your fingers. Add 2 tablespoons of the hot stock and set aside to infuse.

2 Heat the oil in a large saucepan. Add the onion and fry for 5–6 minutes, until golden brown. Add the cumin and fry for a further 20–30 seconds, then stir in the aubergine, red pepper, tomatoes, cinnamon, coriander stalks, saffron liquid and remaining stock. Cover and simmer for 20 minutes.

3 Add the chickpeas to the saucepan and season to taste with salt and pepper. Simmer for a further 5 minutes, removing the lid to reduce and thicken the sauce if necessary.

4 Meanwhile, bring a large, heavy-based saucepan of lightly salted water to the boil. Add the pasta, return to the boil and cook for 8–10 minutes, or until tender but still firm to the bite. Drain and transfer to a warmed serving bowl. Add the sauce and half the coriander leaves, then toss. Garnish with the remaining coriander and serve immediately with the harissa or chilli sauce.

mushroom & ale pot pies

ingredients

serves 2

1 tbsp olive oil

200 g/7 oz button mushrooms, sliced

1 onion, roughly chopped

1 leek, sliced

3 tbsp plain flour, plus extra for dusting

250 ml/9 fl oz vegan stock

250 ml/9 fl oz vegan ale (dark beer)

1 tsp chopped fresh flat-leaf parsley

1 tsp soy sauce

salt and pepper

1 sheet vegan ready-rolled puff pastry

method

1 Preheat the oven to 190°C/375°F/Gas Mark 5.

2 Heat the oil in a large saucepan over a low heat. Fry the mushrooms, onion and leek for 10 minutes, or until the mushrooms have softened. Stir in the flour and cook for a further minute, then gradually whisk in the stock and ale. Stir in the parsley and soy sauce and cook for a further 10 minutes. Remove from the heat, check and adjust the seasoning to taste with salt and pepper, then leave to cool.

3 Place the puff pastry sheet on a floured surface and cut two oval or circular pie tops to fit two 350 ml/12 fl oz pie dishes. Divide the cooled mushroom mixture between the dishes, place the pastry lids on top and transfer to the preheated oven. Bake for 15–20 minutes, or until the pastry is puffy and browned. Leave to cool for 5 minutes, then serve immediately.

smoky bean chimichangas

ingredients

serves 4

2 tbsp olive oil
2 onions, sliced
1 green pepper, deseeded and sliced
1 red pepper, deseeded and sliced
400 g/14 oz canned black beans, drained and rinsed
2 tsp chipotle chilli paste
2 tbsp vegetable oil, plus extra for frying
150 g/5½ oz kale, shredded
juice of 1 orange
4 large soft vegan tortillas
salt and pepper
cooked rice, to serve
carrot salad or salsa, to serve

method

1 Heat the olive oil in a large frying pan over a medium–low heat. Fry the onions and peppers for 10–12 minutes, or until the onions are translucent but the peppers are still quite firm. Stir in the drained beans and chipotle paste, cook for a further minute, and then remove from the heat.

2 Heat the vegetable oil in a small wok over a high heat. Stir-fry the shredded kale with the orange juice for 4 minutes, or until wilted. Season to taste with salt and pepper.

3 Divide the cooked kale between the tortillas, making a neat pile in the middle of each flatbread. Top the greens with a layer of the bean mixture. Then carefully fold up the sides of the tortillas to make parcels.

4 Heat a small amount of vegetable oil in a large frying pan over a medium heat. Fry the chimichanga parcels briefly on both sides (starting with the side where the folds are visible) until crisp and golden. Serve immediately, with rice and salad or salsa on the side.

spicy stuffed peppers

ingredients

serves 4

4 assorted coloured peppers
3 sprays of olive oil spray
1 onion, finely chopped
2 garlic cloves, chopped
2.5-cm/1-inch piece fresh ginger,
    peeled and grated
1–2 fresh serrano chillies,
    deseeded and chopped
1 tsp ground cumin
1 tsp ground coriander
85 g/3 oz cooked brown
    basmati rice
1 large carrot, about 115 g/
    4 oz, grated
1 large courgette, about
    85 g/3 oz, grated
25 g/1 oz ready-to-eat dried
    apricots, finely chopped
1 tbsp chopped fresh coriander
150 ml/5 fl oz water
pepper
fresh herbs, to garnish

method

1 Preheat the oven to 190°C/375°F/Gas Mark 5. Cut the tops off the peppers and reserve. Discard the seeds from each pepper. Place the peppers in a large bowl and cover with boiling water. Leave to soak for 10 minutes then drain and reserve.

2 Place a large frying pan over a medium heat and spray with the oil. Add the onion, garlic, ginger and chillies and fry for 3 minutes, stirring frequently. Sprinkle in the ground spices and continue to cook for a further 2 minutes.

3 Remove the pan from the heat and stir in the rice, carrot, courgette, apricots, chopped coriander and pepper to taste. Stir well, then use to stuff the peppers.

4 Place the stuffed peppers in an ovenproof dish large enough to allow the peppers to stand upright. Put the reserved tops in position. Pour the water around their bases, cover loosely with the lid or foil and bake in the preheated oven for 25–30 minutes, or until piping hot. Serve garnished with herbs.

asparagus & walnut lasagne

ingredients

serves 4

175 g/6 oz asparagus, trimmed

3 tbsp olive oil

70 g/2½ oz spring onions, chopped

2 garlic cloves, chopped

4 tbsp plain flour

850 ml/1½ pints unsweetened soya milk

1 tsp soy sauce

100 g/3½ oz walnuts, roughly chopped, plus 10 g/¼ oz finely chopped

6 vegan dried lasagne sheets

salt and pepper

method

1 Preheat the oven to 180°C/350°F/Gas Mark 4.

2 Bring a large saucepan of salted water to the boil. Add the asparagus and boil for 6–10 minutes, until tender: do not overcook. Drain and refresh with cold water.

3 Heat the oil in a large frying pan over a medium heat. Fry the spring onions and garlic for 3 minutes, then stir in the flour and cook for a further minute. Gradually add the soya milk, whisking constantly and keeping the mixture just on the boil. When all the soya milk has been added, boil for a further minute or two until the mixture has thickened. Remove from the heat, stir in the soy, and season to taste with salt and pepper.

4 Arrange half of the asparagus in the bottom of a 24 x 18-cm/9½ x 7-inch baking dish. Sprinkle half of the chopped walnuts on top, then pour over a third of the milk sauce. Cover with three lasagne sheets, then repeat with the remaining asparagus, chopped walnuts and another third of the remaining sauce. Cover with the three remaining lasagne sheets. Finally, pour over the remaining sauce and sprinkle over the finely chopped walnuts. Season with pepper.

5 Bake in the preheated oven for 25 minutes, or until the lasagne sheets are cooked and the top of the dish is browning. Leave to cool for 5 minutes, then serve.

sweet potato & lentil stew

ingredients

serves 4

2 tbsp olive oil
350 g/12 oz sweet potato, cut into
    1-cm/½-inch cubes
1 onion, chopped
1 carrot, chopped
1 leek, sliced
1 bay leaf
85 g/3 oz Puy lentils
700 ml/1¼ pints vegan stock
1 tbsp chopped fresh sage
salt and pepper

method

1 Heat the oil in a large saucepan or stockpot over a low heat. Gently fry the sweet potato, onion, carrot, leek and bay leaf for 5 minutes.

2 Stir in the lentils, stock and sage, and bring to the boil. Reduce the heat and simmer for 20 minutes, or until the lentils are tender but not disintegrating.

3 Season to taste with salt and pepper, then remove and discard the bay leaf. Serve immediately.

teriyaki tofu noodles

ingredients

serves 2

140 g/5 oz vegan dried noodles
200 g/7 oz firm tofu, drained
2 tbsp sunflower oil or
    vegetable oil
1 red pepper, deseeded and
    thinly sliced
140 g/5 oz baby corn, cut in half
    lengthways
200 g/7 oz choi sum, cut into
    4-cm/1½-inch pieces
salt

sauce

3 tbsp tamari or dark soy sauce
3 tbsp rice wine
2 tbsp light agave nectar
1 tbsp cornflour
1 tbsp finely grated fresh ginger
1–2 garlic cloves, crushed
250 ml/9 fl oz water

method

1 Bring a large saucepan of lightly salted water to the boil. Add the noodles, bring back to the boil and cook for 4 minutes, or until tender but still firm to the bite. Drain.

2 Meanwhile, cut the tofu into 15-mm/⁵/₈-inch slices and then into bite-sized pieces. Pat dry on plenty of kitchen paper. Heat a non-stick or well-seasoned frying pan over a medium–low heat, then add the tofu and cook for 3 minutes, without moving the pieces around the pan, until golden brown underneath. Turn and cook for a further 2–3 minutes on the other side. Transfer to a plate.

3 To make the sauce, mix the tamari, rice wine, agave, cornflour, ginger and garlic together in a jug until well blended, then stir in the water. Set aside.

4 Heat the oil in a wok or a large, heavy-based frying pan. Add the pepper and baby corn, and stir-fry for 3 minutes. Add the choi sum and stir-fry for a further 2 minutes. Pour in the sauce and heat, stirring constantly, until it boils and thickens. Add the noodles and tofu and toss together over the heat for a further 1–2 minutes until heated through. Serve immediately.

pumpkin & tomato spaghetti

ingredients

serves 4

600 g/1 lb 5 oz pumpkin or
butternut squash, cut into
bite-sized pieces
2 red onions, cut into wedges
1 tbsp olive oil
15 sun-dried tomatoes in oil
350 g/12 oz vegan dried spaghetti
salt and pepper
fresh basil leaves, to garnish

method

1 Preheat the oven to 180°C/350°F/Gas Mark 4.

2 Toss the pumpkin and onion together with the olive oil. Place in a roasting tin and roast in the preheated oven for 25–30 minutes, or until tender. Leave to cool for 5 minutes.

3 Cut the sun-dried tomatoes into small pieces and stir into the roasted vegetables. Season to taste with salt and pepper.

4 Bring a large saucepan of salted water to the boil. Add the spaghetti, return to the boil and cook for 8–10 minutes, or until tender but still firm to the bite.

5 Drain the spaghetti well and divide between four warmed serving plates. Top with the vegetables and garnish with fresh basil leaves. Serve immediately.

bean & vegetable chilli

ingredients

serves 4

4 tbsp vegan stock

1 onion, roughly chopped

1 green pepper, deseeded and finely chopped

1 red pepper, deseeded and finely chopped

1 tsp finely chopped garlic

1 tsp finely chopped fresh ginger

2 tsp ground cumin

½ tsp chilli powder

2 tbsp tomato purée

400 g/14 oz canned chopped tomatoes

400 g/14 oz canned kidney beans, drained and rinsed

400 g/14 oz canned black-eyed beans, drained and rinsed

salt and pepper

vegan tortilla chips, to serve

method

1 Heat the stock in a large saucepan, add the onion and peppers and simmer for 5 minutes, or until softened.

2 Stir in the garlic, ginger, cumin, chilli powder, tomato purée and tomatoes. Season to taste with salt and pepper and simmer for 10 minutes.

3 Stir in all the beans and simmer for a further 5 minutes, or until heated through. Serve immediately with tortilla chips.

chickpea & cashew nut curry

ingredients

serves 4

150 g/5½ oz potatoes, chopped
    into bite-sized pieces
3 tbsp vegetable oil
1 onion, chopped
2 garlic cloves, chopped
3-cm/1¼-inch piece fresh ginger,
    peeled and finely chopped
1 tsp cumin seeds
1 tsp chilli powder
½ tsp turmeric
½ tsp cinnamon
400 g/14 oz canned chickpeas,
    drained and rinsed
150 g/5½ oz cashew nut halves
350 ml/12 fl oz vegan stock
100 g/3½ oz creamed coconut
chopped fresh coriander, to garnish
cooked rice, to serve

method

1 Place the potatoes in a large saucepan of boiling water
    and cook for 10–15 minutes, until tender but still firm.

2 Heat the oil in a large saucepan over a medium heat.
    Fry the onion, garlic, ginger, cumin seeds, chilli powder,
    turmeric and cinnamon for 5 minutes, or until the
    onion is soft and translucent.

3 Stir in the boiled potatoes, chickpeas and cashews, and
    cook for a further 3 minutes. Stir in the stock and the
    creamed coconut and stir until the coconut melts into
    the dish. Reduce the heat to low and continue to cook
    for 15 minutes, or until thick and creamy.

4 Garnish with coriander and serve immediately with
    cooked rice.

beetroot & seed risotto

ingredients

serves 6

500 g/1 lb 2 oz raw, whole,
    even-sized beetroot, unpeeled
2 tbsp olive oil
1 onion, finely chopped
1 garlic clove, finely chopped
250 g/9 oz risotto rice
800 ml/1¼ pints vegan stock
200 ml/7 fl oz vegan dry white
    wine
salt and pepper

topping

1 tbsp caraway seeds
50 g/1¾ oz fresh white vegan
    breadcrumbs
½ tsp caster sugar
1 tbsp vegetable oil

method

1 Place the beetroot in a large saucepan, cover with water and bring to the boil. Cook for 45 minutes, or until the beetroot is soft and can be pierced with a fork. Drain in a colander and peel the beetroot under cold running water – you should be able to slide the skin off. Trim away any stubborn skin with a knife and set aside.

2 Preheat the oven to 180°C/350°F/Gas Mark 4. Heat the oil in a large ovenproof casserole over a medium heat. Fry the onion and garlic for 3–4 minutes, or until translucent. Stir in the rice, stock and 150 ml/5 fl oz of the wine, cover and transfer to the preheated oven. Cook for 30 minutes, until the rice is tender.

3 To make the topping, crush the caraway seeds with a rolling pin and then mix all the topping ingredients together in a small bowl. Transfer to a small frying pan and fry, stirring constantly, over a medium heat for 2–3 minutes. Tip the topping onto a plate to cool.

4 Process approximately a quarter of the beetroot to a smooth purée in a food processor. Chop the remaining beetroot finely. Stir the chopped and puréed beetroot into the risotto along with the remaining wine, and season to taste with salt and pepper. Divide the risotto between six warmed serving plates, sprinkle some of the crumbs on top of each and serve immediately.

wild mushroom fusilli

ingredients

serves 4

400 g/14 oz vegan dried fusilli
60 g/2¼ oz hazelnuts
4 tbsp olive oil
1 onion, chopped
4 garlic cloves, chopped
300 g/10½ oz mixed wild
    mushrooms (such as oyster or
    chestnut), roughly chopped
4 tbsp finely chopped fresh
    flat-leaf parsley
salt and pepper

method

1 Bring a large saucepan of lightly salted water to the boil. Add the fusilli, bring back to the boil and cook for 10–12 minutes, or until tender but still firm to the bite.

2 Dry roast the hazelnuts in a small, heavy-based frying pan for 3–4 minutes, or until the skins begin to brown. Turn them out of the pan onto a damp, clean tea towel, fold the tea towel over the nuts and roll them on the work surface to remove most of the skins. Chop the nuts roughly.

3 Heat the oil in a large saucepan over a medium heat. Fry the onion, garlic and mushrooms for 5 minutes, or until beginning to brown. Stir in the chopped nuts and continue to cook for another minute. Season to taste with salt and pepper.

4 Drain the pasta and toss together with the mushroom mixture and the fresh parsley to mix thoroughly. Serve immediately.

carrot & coriander sausage & mash

ingredients

serves 4

sausages

1 tbsp olive oil
25 g/1 oz spring onions, chopped
1 garlic clove, chopped
½ fresh red chilli, deseeded and
    finely chopped
1 tsp ground cumin
450 g/1 lb carrot, grated
½ tsp salt
3 tbsp crunchy peanut butter
25 g/1 oz finely chopped fresh
    coriander, plus extra to garnish
100 g/3½ oz fresh brown vegan
    breadcrumbs
plain flour, for dusting
vegetable oil, for frying

mash

900 g/2 lb floury potatoes,
    chopped
3 tbsp unsweetened soya milk
55 g/2 oz vegan margarine
salt and pepper

method

1 To make the sausages, heat the olive oil in a large saucepan over a medium heat. Fry the spring onions, garlic, chilli and cumin for 2 minutes. Stir in the carrots and salt and mix well. Cover the pan and cook on a very low heat for 6–8 minutes, or until the carrot is tender.

2 Transfer the carrot mixture to a large mixing bowl and mix in the peanut butter and coriander, ensuring that the ingredients are thoroughly combined. Allow the mixture to cool, and then mix in the breadcrumbs.

3 On a floured surface, form the mixture into eight large sausages. Leave to chill in the refrigerator for up to an hour. Heat the vegetable oil in a frying pan over a medium heat and fry the sausages gently for 10 minutes, turning occasionally, until browned.

4 Meanwhile, bring a large saucepan of lightly salted water to the boil. Add the potatoes, bring back to the boil and cook for 15–20 minutes, or until cooked through and fluffy. Transfer to a mixing bowl, add the milk and vegan margarine and mash the mixture thoroughly until all lumps are removed. Season to taste with salt and pepper.

5 Place the mashed potato on warmed plates and top with the sausages. Garnish with coriander and serve.

thai red curry

ingredients

serves 4

2 tbsp groundnut oil or
   vegetable oil
2 onions, thinly sliced
1 bunch of fine asparagus spears
400 ml/14 fl oz coconut milk
2 tbsp vegan Thai red curry paste
3 fresh kaffir lime leaves
225 g/8 oz baby spinach leaves
2 heads pak choi, chopped
1 small head Chinese leaves,
   shredded
handful of fresh coriander, chopped
cooked rice, to serve

method

1 Heat a wok over a medium–high heat and add the
   oil. Add the onions and asparagus and stir-fry for
   1–2 minutes.

2 Add the coconut milk, curry paste and lime leaves and
   bring gently to the boil, stirring occasionally.

3 Add the spinach, pak choi and Chinese leaves and
   cook, stirring, for 2–3 minutes, until wilted. Add the
   coriander and stir well. Serve immediately with freshly
   cooked rice.

potato, broccoli & peanut bake

ingredients

serves 4

450 g/1 lb new potatoes, sliced
1 tbsp olive oil
½ small onion, finely chopped
400 ml/14 fl oz coconut milk
8 tbsp crunchy peanut butter
1 tbsp soy sauce
2 tsp sugar
½ tsp dried red chilli flakes
200 g/7 oz broccoli florets
60 g/2¼ oz unsalted peanuts
2 tsp melted vegan margarine
salt and pepper

method

1 Preheat the oven to 190°C/375°F/Gas Mark 5.

2 Bring a large saucepan of lightly salted water to the boil. Add the potatoes, bring back to the boil and cook for 8–10 minutes, or until slightly softened. Drain and set aside.

3 Heat the oil in a saucepan over a medium heat. Fry the onion for 2 minutes, then stir in the coconut milk, peanut butter, soy sauce, sugar and chilli flakes. Bring to the boil and stir well to ensure the ingredients are well combined. Reduce the heat and simmer for 5 minutes.

4 Meanwhile, place the broccoli in a steamer and lightly steam for 4–5 minutes, or until just tender.

5 Stir the broccoli and peanuts into the sauce, season to taste and transfer to a wide, square baking dish.

6 Cover the mixture with the cooked potato slices, dot with the melted margarine and season with pepper. Bake in the preheated oven for 20–25 minutes, or until the potatoes are golden. Leave to cool for 5 minutes before serving.

kale & artichoke gnocchi

ingredients

serves 4

200 g/7 oz shredded kale
2 tbsp olive oil
1 onion, chopped
400 g/14 oz canned artichoke
    hearts, quartered
2 garlic cloves, chopped
1 tsp red chilli flakes
juice of ½ lemon
2 tbsp pine nuts
salt

gnocchi

675 g/1 lb 8 oz even-sized baking
    potatoes
250 g/9 oz plain flour, plus extra
    for dusting
2 tbsp olive oil

method

1 To make the gnocchi, preheat the oven to 230°C/450°F/ Gas Mark 8. Place the potatoes on a baking sheet and bake until fluffy all the way through – 45 minutes to an hour depending on the size of the potatoes. Leave to cool, then peel and mash the flesh with a potato ricer or masher, until very smooth. There should be no 'bits'.

2 Turn the potato mash onto a floured board and knead, working in the flour and oil, for 5 minutes. Divide the mixture into four and roll each into a long snake. Use a knife to cut into pieces (around 2 cm/¾ inch long).

3 Bring a large saucepan of salted water to the boil. Add the kale, return to the boil and cook for 6–8 minutes. Drain and firmly press out any excess water.

4 Heat the oil in a frying pan over a high heat. Add the onion and fry for 3 minutes, then stir in the artichokes, garlic and chilli. Cook for a further minute, then stir in the kale, lemon juice and pine nuts. Set aside.

5 Bring a large pan of salted water to the boil. Add a small batch of the gnocchi, return to the boil and cook for 2–3 minutes, until they float on the surface of the water. Continue to cook batches of the remaining gnocchi in the same way. Mix the gnocchi thoroughly with the kale mixture and serve immediately.

raw shoots & seeds super salad

ingredients

serves 6

225 g/8 oz mixed sprouted seeds
    and beans (such as alfalfa,
    mung beans, soy beans,
    aduki beans, chickpeas and
    radish seeds)
30 g/1 oz pumpkin seeds
30 g/1 oz sunflower seeds
30 g/1 oz sesame seeds
1 small apple
70 g/2½ oz dried apricots
grated rind and juice of 1 lemon
50 g/1¾ oz walnuts, roughly
    chopped
2 tbsp vegan omega-rich oil

method

1 In a large mixing bowl, combine the sprouts and seeds.
    Core and chop the apple and chop the apricots into
    small pieces. Stir the fruit into the bowl, then stir in the
    lemon rind and walnuts.

2 Make a dressing by mixing the lemon juice with the oil
    in a small bowl using a fork to thoroughly combine.

3 Stir the dressing into the salad and serve immediately.

sichuan mixed vegetables

ingredients

serves 4

2 tbsp chilli oil
4 garlic cloves, crushed
5-cm/2-inch piece fresh ginger,
    peeled and grated
250 g/9 oz carrots, cut into
    thin strips
1 red pepper, deseeded and cut
    into thin strips
150 g/5½ oz shiitake mushrooms,
    sliced
150 g/5½ oz mangetout
3 tbsp soy sauce
3 tbsp crunchy peanut butter
350 g/12 oz beansprouts
cooked rice, to serve

method

1 Heat the chilli oil in a preheated wok and fry the garlic,
   ginger and carrots for 3 minutes. Add the red pepper
   and stir-fry for another 2 minutes.

2 Add the mushrooms and mangetout and stir-fry for
   1 minute.

3 In a small bowl, mix together the soy sauce and peanut
   butter until combined.

4 Using a wooden spoon, make a space in the centre
   of the stir-fried vegetables so that the base of the
   wok is visible. Pour in the sauce and bring to the boil,
   stirring all the time until it starts to thicken. Add the
   beansprouts and toss the vegetables to coat
   thoroughly with the sauce.

5 Transfer to a serving dish and serve immediately with
   freshly cooked rice.

golden vegetable crumble

ingredients

serves 4

2 tbsp olive oil

200 g/7 oz butternut squash, chopped

150 g/5½ oz sweet potato, chopped

1 onion, chopped

2 carrots, sliced

1 tsp cinnamon

¼ tsp turmeric

600 ml/1 pint vegan stock

70 g/2½ oz baby corn, halved lengthways

topping

70 g/2½ oz vegan margarine

100 g/3½ oz plain flour

70 g/2½ oz walnuts, roughly chopped

4 tbsp porridge oats

salt and pepper

method

1 Preheat the oven to 200°C/400°F/Gas Mark 6.

2 Heat the oil in a large saucepan over a medium heat. Fry the butternut squash, sweet potato, onion and carrots for 5 minutes. Stir in the cinnamon and turmeric and cook for 2 more minutes. Pour in the stock, reduce the heat and simmer, stirring frequently, for 10 minutes. Stir in the baby corn.

3 To make the crumble topping, rub the margarine into the flour in a mixing bowl, until it forms a breadcrumb consistency. Stir in the walnuts and oats until mixed thoroughly then season to taste with salt and pepper.

4 Transfer the vegetables into a 20-cm/8-inch square baking dish. Top with the crumble mixture and bake in the preheated oven for 20 minutes, or until warmed through and golden. Leave to cool for 5 minutes and then serve immediately.

barbecue tofu kebabs

ingredients

makes 6

400 g/14 oz firm tofu
3 red onions, quartered
12 button mushrooms

marinade

250 ml/9 fl oz passata
3 tbsp cider vinegar
2 tbsp dark brown sugar
2 garlic cloves, finely chopped
¼ tsp salt
¼ tsp chilli powder
¼ tsp smoked paprika

method

1 To make the barbecue marinade, combine all of the ingredients in a saucepan, stir and place over a low heat. Simmer for 10 minutes.

2 Drain the tofu and press it with kitchen paper to remove any excess water. Cut it into nine squares, and then cut each square in half to make 18 pieces.

3 Arrange the tofu pieces, onion pieces and mushrooms in a large baking dish and pour over the warm marinade. Stir the mixture carefully to ensure that everything is well coated, but take care not to break the tofu. Cover and leave to cool. The mixture can then be refrigerated until needed. Allow the tofu and vegetables to marinate for at least 2 hours.

4 Preheat the grill to high. If you are using wooden skewers, presoak them in water for 10 minutes before making up the kebabs. Thread two mushrooms, two pieces of onion and three pieces of tofu onto six presoaked wooden skewers. Baste with the remaining sauce and place under the preheated grill or on a barbecue, turning occasionally, until well browned and sizzling. Serve immediately.

chunky lentil & brazil nut roast

ingredients

serves 6

vegan margarine, for greasing
225 g/8 oz red lentils
1 bay leaf
2 tbsp olive oil
1 onion, finely chopped
2 garlic cloves, finely chopped
1 carrot, finely chopped
300 g/10½ oz Brazil nuts
1 tbsp tomato purée
1 tbsp soy sauce
115 g/4 oz fresh white vegan
    breadcrumbs
1 tbsp dried oregano
steamed green vegetables, to serve

method

1 Preheat the oven to 190°C/375°F/Gas Mark 5. Grease and line a 900 g/2 lb loaf tin.

2 Place the lentils and bay leaf in a large saucepan with 375 ml/13 fl oz of water. Bring to the boil and then simmer for 25 minutes, or until the lentils are cooked to a mush. Remove and discard the bay leaf and set aside.

3 Heat the oil in a large frying pan over a medium heat. Fry the onion, garlic and carrot for 3 minutes. Roughly chop one third of the Brazil nuts. Place the remaining nuts in a food processor and pulse until processed to a powder. Transfer the onion mixture into a large mixing bowl with the ground and chopped nuts, lentils, tomato purée, soy sauce, breadcrumbs and oregano. Mix thoroughly and press into the prepared tin.

4 Bake in the preheated oven for 25 minutes. Leave to cool a little in the tin before turning out and slicing. Serve hot or cold with steamed green vegetables.

variation

Add a colourful filling – half-fill the tin with the nut mixture, then add a layer of chopped sun-dried tomatoes, chopped roasted red peppers and chopped fresh herbs, then add the rest of the nut mixture and bake as in step 4.

artichoke & tomato pithivier

ingredients

serves 6

1 tbsp olive oil, plus extra for
greasing
1 onion, sliced
2 garlic cloves, finely chopped
85 g/3 oz sun-dried tomatoes in
oil, roughly chopped
150 g/5½ oz artichoke hearts in
oil, roughly chopped
1 tbsp chopped fresh tarragon
1 tsp sun-dried tomato purée
4 tbsp vegan dry white wine
1 pack vegan ready-rolled
puff pastry
plain flour, for dusting

method

1 Preheat the oven to 200°C/400°F/Gas Mark 6. Lightly
grease a baking sheet.

2 Heat the oil in a large frying pan over a medium heat.
Fry the onion for 5 minutes, or until softened. Stir in the
garlic, sun-dried tomatoes, artichoke hearts, tarragon,
tomato purée and wine. Mix everything together well
and cook for a further 5 minutes. Remove from the heat
and leave to cool for 5 minutes.

3 Place the puff pastry sheet on a floured surface. Using
a sharp knife, cut two circles, one 23 cm/9 inch in
diameter and one 20 cm/8 inch in diameter.

4 Place the smaller circle of pastry on the prepared
baking sheet and top with the filling, leaving a
2.5-cm/1-inch border around the edge. Put the
larger circle of pastry on top, press the edges together
firmly to seal and then fold in the edge and crimp
decoratively with your fingers or a fork. Using the tip
of a sharp knife, make a little hole in the top of the
pithivier to allow steam to escape.

5 Bake in the preheated oven for 20 minutes, or until
golden. Serve immediately.

hot tofu fajitas

ingredients

serves 4

fajita spice
¼ tsp garlic powder
¼ tsp onion powder
¼ tsp cayenne pepper
¼ tsp dried oregano
¼ tsp ground allspice
1 tbsp plain flour

200 g/7 oz firm tofu
3 tbsp vegetable oil
1 onion, thickly sliced
1 red pepper, deseeded and sliced
1 yellow pepper, deseeded and sliced
4 soft vegan tortillas, warmed
salsa and lime wedges, to serve

method

1 Drain the tofu and press with kitchen paper to remove any excess water. Cut into slices approximately 1 cm/½ inch thick.

2 Combine the fajita spice ingredients in a small bowl and spread onto a large plate. Dip the tofu into the spices, coating both sides of each slice with the mixture.

3 Heat 2 tablespoons of the vegetable oil in a large frying pan over a medium heat. Fry the tofu slices for 5 minutes, turning carefully once or twice, until browned and crisp.

4 In a small bowl, toss the onion and peppers in the remaining vegetable oil. Fry in a hot griddle pan for 6–8 minutes. Try not to move the vegetables too often, so that you get some distinctive stripes.

5 Serve the warm tofu and the vegetables in bowls with the tortillas on separate plates, allowing everybody to assemble their own fajita. Serve with salsa and lime wedges, for squeezing over.

smoky mushroom burgers

ingredients

serves 6

425 g/15 oz canned red kidney
    beans, drained and rinsed
2 tbsp sunflower oil or vegetable
    oil, plus extra for brushing
1 onion, finely chopped
115 g/4 oz mushrooms, finely
    chopped
1 large carrot, coarsely grated
2 tsp smoked paprika
70 g/2½ oz porridge oats
3 tbsp dark soy sauce
2 tbsp tomato purée
30 g/1 oz fresh coriander, including
    stalks, chopped
3 tbsp plain flour
salt and pepper

to serve

vegan hamburger rolls
salad leaves
sliced avocado
tomato salsa or relish

method

1 Place the beans in a large bowl and mash thoroughly
with a potato masher. Heat the oil in a frying pan, add
the onion and fry for 2 minutes until translucent. Add
the mushrooms, carrot and paprika and fry for a further
4 minutes until the vegetables are soft.

2 Add the fried vegetables to the beans with the oats,
soy sauce, tomato purée and coriander. Season with
salt and pepper and mix well. Divide into six equal
portions and shape into burgers, then turn in the
flour to coat lightly.

3 Preheat a griddle pan until smoking. Lightly brush the
tops of the burgers with oil, then place oiled side down
on the pan. Cook over a medium heat for 2–3 minutes
until lightly charred underneath. Lightly brush the tops
with oil, turn and cook for a further 2–3 minutes on the
other side. Serve hot in soft rolls with salad leaves,
avocado slices and salsa.

desserts

fruit salad with ice cream

ingredients

serves 4

ice cream

2 tbsp arrowroot powder
250 ml/9 fl oz soya milk
500 ml/18 fl oz soya cream
150 g/5½ oz caster sugar
1 tbsp vanilla extract

fruit salad

300 g/10½ oz mixed summer fruit
    (strawberries, raspberries,
    blueberries, peaches,
    nectarines, kiwi fruit)
fresh mint leaves, to garnish

method

1 In a small bowl, mix the arrowroot with sufficient soya milk to make a smooth, runny mixture and set aside.

2 Put the remaining soya milk, soya cream and sugar into a large saucepan and bring to the boil, stirring to ensure that the sugar is dissolved. Once boiling point is reached, take the pan off the heat and stir in the arrowroot mixture and the vanilla extract. Leave to cool.

3 Transfer to an ice-cream maker and churn according to the manufacturer's instructions. Alternatively, pour the cooled mixture into a shallow freezerproof container and place in the freezer. Leave to freeze until not quite set, then take out of the freezer, stir and freeze again until firm.

4 Rinse or peel the fruit and chop into bite-sized pieces, if preferred. Serve with the ice cream, garnished with one or two fresh mint leaves.

sparkling wine sorbet

ingredients

serves 4

150 g/5½ oz caster sugar
150 ml/5 fl oz water
thinly pared strip of lemon zest
juice of 1 lemon
350 ml/12 fl oz vegan sparkling
    wine
grapes and fresh mint sprigs,
    to decorate

method

1 Place the sugar and water in a pan with the lemon zest.
  Stir over a low heat until the sugar dissolves, then boil
  for 2–3 minutes to reduce by half. Leave to cool and
  remove the lemon zest.

2 Combine the syrup with the lemon juice and wine,
  then churn the mixture in an ice-cream maker
  following the manufacturer's instructions. Alternatively,
  pour the cooled mixture into a shallow freezerproof
  container and freeze, uncovered, whisking at hourly
  intervals until frozen.

3 When ready to serve, leave at room temperature
  to soften slightly, then scoop the sorbet into
  sundae glasses. Decorate with grapes and mint sprigs.

raw chocolate ice cream

ingredients

serves 4

3 bananas (approx. 300 g/10½ oz)
3 tbsp raw cocoa powder
1 tbsp agave nectar

method

1 Peel the bananas and cut them into 2-cm/¾-inch pieces. Place in a freezer bag and freeze for 3 hours.

2 Take the bananas from the freezer and place in a food processor or blender with the cocoa powder and agave nectar. Process until smooth. Serve immediately or refreeze for a firmer consistency.

green tea & hazelnut ice cream

ingredients

serves 6

400 ml/14 fl oz canned
  coconut milk
200 g/7 oz creamed coconut
200 g/7 oz caster sugar
3 tsp green tea powder
50 g/1¾ oz roast hazelnuts,
  chopped

method

1 Place the coconut milk and creamed coconut in a medium saucepan over a medium heat. Stir continuously, until both ingredients have blended together.

2 Whisk in the sugar and green tea powder. Stir in the chopped hazelnuts and set aside to cool to room temperature.

3 Transfer to an ice-cream maker and churn according to the manufacturer's instructions. Alternatively, pour the cooled mixture into a shallow freezerproof container and place in the freezer. Leave to freeze until not quite set, then remove from the freezer, stir and freeze again until firm. Store in the freezer until required.

baked plums with port

ingredients

serves 4

8 large plums
1 cinnamon stick
2 strips pared orange rind
25 g/1 oz soft light brown sugar
2 tbsp light agave nectar
200 ml/7 fl oz vegan port

method

1 Preheat the oven to 180°C/350°F/Gas Mark 4. Halve and stone the plums.

2 Place the plum halves cut side up in a small baking dish with the cinnamon stick and orange rind. Sprinkle over the sugar. Mix together the agave and port and pour around the plums.

3 Bake in the preheated oven for 30–40 minutes, or until the plums are soft. Leave to cool for 5 minutes, then pour off the liquid into a small saucepan.

4 Bring the liquid to the boil, then simmer for 5–10 minutes, or until syrupy and reduced by about one third. Pour the syrup over the plums. Serve immediately.

coconut rice pudding

ingredients

serves 4

5 cardamom pods
100 g/3½ oz short grain
   pudding rice
600 ml/1 pint soya milk
400 ml/14 fl oz coconut milk
55 g/2 oz caster sugar
pinch of saffron
2 tbsp flaked almonds

method

1 Crack open the cardamom pods and remove the seeds. Crush the seeds in a pestle and mortar or with a rolling pin. Place the rice, soya milk, coconut milk, sugar, crushed cardamom seeds and saffron in a large saucepan over a low heat. Simmer for 40 minutes, stirring frequently, until the mixture is thick and creamy.

2 Toast the flaked almonds in a dry frying pan over a high heat for 2–3 minutes, or until lightly golden.

3 Serve the rice pudding hot or cold, topped with the toasted almonds.

blueberry strudel

ingredients

serves 4–6

200 g/7 oz blueberries
1 tbsp cornflour
100 g/3½ oz caster sugar
plain flour, for dusting
270 g/9½ oz vegan filo pastry
50 g/1¾ oz vegan margarine,
    melted and cooled
icing sugar, to serve

method

1 Preheat the oven to 190°C/375°F/Gas Mark 5. Line a baking sheet with baking paper.

2 In a medium bowl, mix together the blueberries, cornflour and sugar.

3 Place two sheets of filo pastry on a floured board, overlapping them slightly. Brush them with melted margarine and cover with two more sheets. Brush these with margarine and top with a further two sheets of pastry.

4 Place the fruit mixture in a line close to one long edge of the pastry. Starting at that edge, carefully roll up the pastry, folding in the ends as you roll.

5 Transfer the strudel to the prepared baking sheet, brush the surface with the remaining melted margarine and bake in the preheated oven for 20 minutes, or until golden. Dust with icing sugar before serving warm or cold.

spiced pumpkin tartlets

ingredients

serves 4

400 g/14 oz pumpkin, cut into
   1-cm/½-inch pieces
10 g/¼ oz vegan margarine,
   melted, plus extra for greasing
1 tbsp maple syrup
10 g/¼ oz preserved stem ginger
   in syrup, finely chopped
¼ tsp cinnamon
¼ tsp allspice
135 g/4¾ oz vegan filo pastry
2 tbsp rapeseed oil
icing sugar, to serve

method

1 Preheat the oven to 190°C/375°F/Gas Mark 5. Lightly
grease four 10-cm/4-inch tartlet tins.

2 Place the pumpkin on a baking sheet and dot with
the margarine. Roast in the preheated oven for
5 minutes, then stir and return to the oven for a
further 20 minutes, or until the pumpkin is beginning
to brown. Stir in the maple syrup, chopped ginger,
cinnamon and allspice, and cook for a further
5 minutes. Leave to cool.

3 Cut the filo pastry into twelve 10-cm/4-inch squares.
Brush four with rapeseed oil. Place a second sheet of
pastry on top of each, at an angle to the first so that
the points of the squares do not align – you are aiming
to create a star shape. Brush with oil again and finish
with the remaining pastry sheets to make four stacks,
each with three layers. Transfer the pastry stacks into
the prepared tartlet tins, press down gently, and bake
for 8–10 minutes, or until crisp and golden.

4 Fill the pastry cases with the pumpkin mixture. Dust
with icing sugar and serve immediately.

baked apples

ingredients

serves 4

4 cooking apples
1 tbsp lemon juice
50 g/1¾ oz blueberries
50 g/1¾ oz raisins
25 g/1 oz mixed nuts, chopped
    and toasted
½ tsp ground cinnamon
2 tbsp soft brown sugar
275 ml/9½ fl oz vegan red wine
2 tsp cornflour
4 tsp water

method

1 Preheat the oven to 200°C/400°F/Gas Mark 6. Using a sharp knife, score a line around the centre of each apple. Core the apples, then brush the centres with the lemon juice to prevent discoloration. Transfer them to a small roasting tin.

2 Place the blueberries and raisins in a bowl, then add the nuts, cinnamon and sugar. Mix together well. Pile the mixture into the centres of the apples, then pour over the wine.

3 Transfer the stuffed apples to the preheated oven and bake for 40–45 minutes, or until tender. Remove from the oven, then lift the apples out of the roasting tin and keep them warm.

4 Blend the cornflour with the water, then add the mixture to the cooking juices in the roasting tin. Transfer to the hob and cook over a medium heat, stirring, until thickened. Remove from the heat and pour over the apples. Serve immediately.

raspberry chocolate cake

ingredients

serves 12

vegan margarine, for greasing
300 g/10½ oz plain flour
50 g/1¾ oz cocoa powder
1 tsp baking powder
1 tsp bicarbonate of soda
½ tsp salt
300 g/10½ oz granulated sugar
375 ml/13 fl oz soya milk
125 ml/4 fl oz rapeseed oil
7 tbsp seedless raspberry jam
1 tsp vanilla extract

icing

40 ml/1½ fl oz soya milk
85 g/3 oz vegan dark chocolate,
    broken into small pieces
60 g/2¼ oz icing sugar
1 tbsp maple syrup
fresh raspberries, to decorate

method

1 Preheat the oven to 180°C/350°F/Gas Mark 4. Grease a 23-cm/9-inch cake tin and line with baking paper.

2 Sift the flour, cocoa, baking powder and bicarbonate of soda into a large mixing bowl and stir in the salt and sugar. Pour the soya milk into a medium saucepan and add the oil, raspberry jam and vanilla extract. Place over a medium heat and whisk to combine. Stir into the dry ingredients and mix thoroughly.

3 Transfer to the prepared cake tin and bake in the preheated oven for 45 minutes, or until a skewer inserted into the centre comes out clean. Leave to cool completely on a wire rack before icing.

4 To make the icing, heat the soya milk in a small saucepan over a medium heat until it reaches boiling point, then drop the chocolate into the pan and stir until completely melted. Remove from the heat and whisk in the icing sugar and maple syrup. Set aside to cool before icing the cake, using a palette knife. Top with a few fresh raspberries before slicing and serving.

variation

For a chocolate and orange cake, substitute orange marmalade for the raspberry jam and decorate with segmented oranges dipped in melted vegan chocolate.

mixed berry bundt cake

ingredients

serves 12

350 g/12 oz plain flour,
    plus extra for dusting
2 tsp baking powder
1 tsp bicarbonate of soda
400 g/14 oz caster sugar
55 g/2 oz desiccated coconut
500 ml/18 fl oz soya milk
150 ml/5 fl oz rapeseed oil,
    plus extra for greasing
2 tsp vanilla extract
1 tsp salt
250 g/9 oz mixed berries, such as
    raspberries, blueberries and
    blackberries, plus extra to serve
icing sugar, to dust
vegan vanilla ice cream, to serve
    (optional)

method

1 Preheat the oven to 180°C/350°F/Gas Mark 4. Grease and flour a 24-cm/9½-inch bundt tin.

2 Sift together the flour, baking powder and bicarbonate of soda into a large bowl and stir in the sugar and coconut. Add the soya milk, oil and vanilla extract. Whisk together until smooth – the mixture will look like a thick batter. Stir in the salt and berries.

3 Pour the batter into the bundt tin. Bake in the preheated oven for 1 hour, or until a skewer inserted into the cake comes out clean. Leave to cool in the tin for 5 minutes before turning out onto a wire rack.

4 When the cake has cooled, dust it with icing sugar and fill the centre with more fresh berries. Slice and serve with a scoop of vegan vanilla ice cream, if desired.

boozy summer pudding

ingredients

serves 6

600 g/1 lb 5 oz mixed redcurrants, blackcurrants, blueberries and raspberries, plus extra to decorate (optional)

3–4 tbsp caster sugar

6 tbsp vegan port

300 g/10½ oz strawberries, hulled and halved or quartered if large

6–7 slices vegan thick white bread, crusts removed

method

1 Place the mixed fruit, two tablespoons of the sugar and half of the port in a saucepan over a low heat. Simmer gently for 3–4 minutes until the fruit starts to release its juices. Remove from the heat. Add the strawberries and stir in the remaining sugar to taste.

2 Line a 1-litre/1¾-pint pudding basin with clingfilm, letting the ends overhang. Tip the fruit into a sieve set over a bowl to catch the juices, then stir the remaining port into the juices. Cut a circle the same size as the bottom of the basin out of one slice of bread. Dip in the juice mixture and place in the bottom of the basin.

3 Reserve one slice of bread. Cut the rest in half slightly on an angle. Dip the pieces one at a time in the juice mixture and place around the sides of the basin, narrowest end down, pushing them together so there aren't any gaps and trimming the final piece of bread to fit. Fill with the fruit then cover with the reserved piece of bread, cut to fit the basin top. Put a small plate on top and weigh it down with a can. Chill overnight. Set aside any remaining juice in the refrigerator.

4 Remove the weight and plate, then cover the pudding with a plate and flip over. Remove the bowl and clingfilm and decorate with extra summer fruits (if using). Serve with any remaining juice.

grilled tropical fruit skewers

ingredients

makes 8

rum sauce
4 tbsp orange juice
3 or 4 strips of orange zest
3 or 4 strips of lemon zest
125 ml/4 fl oz vegan dark rum
30 g/1 oz dark brown sugar
3 cardamom pods, cracked open

selection of tropical fruit (melon, star fruit, orange, kiwi fruit, pineapple, banana, mango)

method

1 Put all of the ingredients for the rum sauce into a small saucepan. Place over a low heat and simmer for 10–15 minutes, or until reduced by half. Use a slotted spoon to remove the zest and cardamom pods. Set aside to reheat when you are ready to serve the skewers.

2 Rinse or peel the fruit and cut into large pieces. If you are using wooden skewers, presoak them in water for 10 minutes before making up the skewers. Assemble eight skewers, allowing 8–10 pieces of fruit per skewer.

3 Preheat the grill to high. Place the skewers under the preheated grill or on a barbecue, turning frequently, until browning and heated through. Serve immediately with the rum sauce.

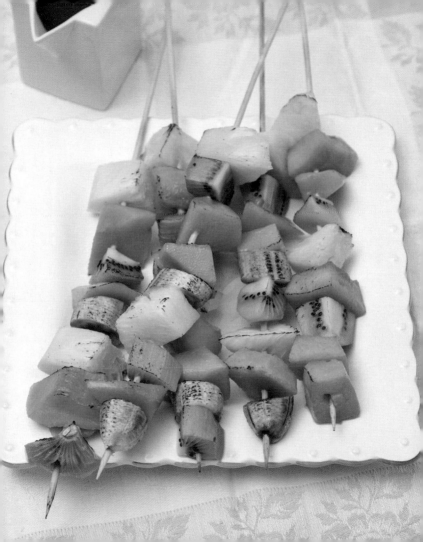

peanut butter cups

ingredients

makes 30

60 g/2¼ oz smooth peanut butter
2 tbsp vegan margarine
25 g/1 oz icing sugar
350 g/12 oz vegan dark chocolate,
    broken into pieces

method

1 Line a mini muffin tray with 30 mini paper cases.

2 Place the peanut butter and 1 tablespoon of the margarine in a small non-metallic bowl. Microwave for 30 seconds to 1 minute, or until softened but not melted. Mix the icing sugar in thoroughly.

3 Place the chocolate and the remaining margarine in a large heatproof bowl set over a pan of simmering water. Stir until completely melted.

4 Put a teaspoonful of melted chocolate into each paper cup, top with half a teaspoon of the peanut butter filling and cover the filling with more melted chocolate. Take care not to overfill the cases. Chill in the refrigerator for 1 hour, or until firm.

pecan & cranberry pie

ingredients

serves 6

dough
50 g/1¾ oz vegan margarine
150 g/5½ oz plain flour, plus extra
    for dusting
15 g/½ oz icing sugar

filling
30 g/1 oz dried cranberries
grated rind and juice of 1 orange
1 tbsp vegan brandy (optional)
125 g/4½ oz pecan nuts
150 ml/5 fl oz maple syrup
100 ml/3½ fl oz soya milk
3 tbsp vanilla extract
1 tsp cinnamon
1 tsp ginger
1 tsp linseed meal
    (ground golden linseeds)

method

1 Preheat the oven to 190°C/375°F/Gas Mark 5.

2 Place the cranberries in a small bowl with the orange juice and brandy, if using. Set aside for at least an hour to plump up.

3 To make the dough, rub the margarine into the flour in a large mixing bowl and then stir in the icing sugar. Gradually add sufficient cold water to make a soft dough. Roll the dough out on a floured board and use it to line a 20-cm/8-inch flan tin. Put the pecans into the pastry case and bake in the preheated oven for 15 minutes.

4 Put the maple syrup, soya milk, vanilla extract, cinnamon, ginger and orange rind into a medium saucepan over a low heat. Simmer gently for 5 minutes then remove from the heat.

5 Remove the pastry case from the oven but leave the oven on. Use a slotted spoon to remove the cranberries from the soaking liquid and arrange them on top of the pecans. Stir the linseed meal into the remaining soaking liquid and then stir this into the maple mixture.

6 Carefully pour the mixture into the pastry case. Return the pie to the oven for a further 30 minutes. Leave to cool before slicing and serving.

rhubarb & plum crumble

ingredients

serves 4

300 g/10½ oz rhubarb, chopped
    into 2.5-cm/1-inch pieces
90 g/3¼ oz caster sugar
450 g/1 lb ripe plums, halved and
    stoned
½ tsp cinnamon

topping

50 g/1¾ oz hazelnuts, chopped
85 g/3 oz vegan margarine
140 g/5 oz plain flour
50 g/1¾ oz caster sugar

method

1 Preheat the oven to 190°C/375°F/Gas Mark 5.

2 Place the rhubarb and 60 g/2¼ oz of the caster sugar in a large lidded saucepan. Place over a very low heat and cook, covered, for 5–8 minutes, or until tender.

3 Transfer the rhubarb to a 20-cm/8-inch square baking dish and spread the plums on top. Sprinkle with the remaining caster sugar sifted with the cinnamon.

4 To make the topping, toast the chopped hazelnuts in a dry frying pan over a high heat for 5 minutes, or until browned.

5 In a large mixing bowl, rub the margarine into the flour to resemble large breadcrumbs and then stir in the sugar and toasted nuts. Cover the fruit with the crumble mixture and bake in the preheated oven for 25–30 minutes, or until browning and bubbling. Leave to cool for 5 minutes then serve immediately.